The BIG Guide to Small Pets

A modern approach for a healthy, fulfilled pet.

ADAM ROGERS

AuthorHouse™ UK Ltd.
500 Avebury Boulevard
Central Milton Keynes, MK9 2BE
www.authorhouse.co.uk
Phone: 08001974150

Looking after any animal requires knowledge, dedication and understanding. Any animal can bite or inflict damage, even with proper handling. The author has made every attempt to offer accurate and reliable information to the best of his knowledge and belief, however it is offered without any guarantee. The author and publishers therefore disclaim any liability incurred in connection with using the information contained in this book.
If you are at all worried about your pet's health, behaviour or wellbeing, it is vitally important that you seek advice from a Veterinarian. The advice and information contained in this book is not intended as an alternative to veterinary advice.

© 2012 Adam Rogers. All rights reserved.

No part of this book may be reproduced, stored in a retrieval system, or transmitted by any means without the written permission of the author.

Published by AuthorHouse 2/21/2012

ISBN: 978-1-4567-8464-5 (sc)

Any people depicted in stock imagery provided by Thinkstock are models, and such images are being used for illustrative purposes only.
Certain stock imagery © Thinkstock.

Because of the dynamic nature of the Internet, any web addresses or links contained in this book may have changed since publication and may no longer be valid. The views expressed in this work are solely those of the author and do not necessarily reflect the views of the publisher, and the publisher hereby disclaims any responsibility for them.

authorHOUSE®

Contents

Introduction iv
Chapter 1 – Choosing your small pet 1
Chapter 2 – Housing your small pet 13
Chapter 3 – Feeding your small pet 22
Chapter 4 – Understanding your pet 37
Chapter 5 – Behaviour problems 50
Chapter 6 – Handling your small pet 60
Chapter 7 – Clicker training your pet 62
Chapter 8 – Getting in TTouch with your small pet 68
Chapter 9 – Common behaviour problems 97
Chapter 10 – When the end comes 121
Contact list and useful sources of information 124
Acknowledgments and thanks 125

Introduction

Caring for any animal in captivity is a huge undertaking; choosing to look after a small pet does not mean less responsibility when it comes to caring for you pet's needs. In fact, small pets often require more time and understanding to ensure that their physical and mental needs are met, than do dogs and cats.

The Big Guide to Small Pets aims to provide you with a new understanding of your pet's behavioural and physical needs to ensure you are providing the correct environment for your pet to be happy and healthy. Many information guides for small pets are outdated and old fashioned, the Big Guide to Small Pets, however, is different; it includes the latest and most up to date information on caring for your small pet's body and mind.

Owning a small pet can provide many hours of enjoyment, but beware! Small pets are living, breathing creatures and their well-being must be paramount. Owning a small pet should be an equal partnership offering enjoyment and quality of life to you both. No animal should be made to live in a barren cage with limited opportunity for physical and mental stimulation and it is down to you as your pet's primary carer to ensure all its needs are met. If you are not prepared to dedicate yourself to caring for your pet for the whole if its life, please think twice before acquiring it. Rescue centres are full to the brim with unwanted small pets and many thousands are needlessly put to sleep across the country, mainly due to a lack of thought or preparation or due to the novelty value wearing off. If you can't commit yourself 100% to your pet then please do not get one, it's not only dogs that are for life, not just for Christmas!

Chapter 1 – Choosing your small pet

Making the right decision

Why choose a small pet?

In our increasingly busy world with longer and longer working hours, many people are turning to smaller pets that more easily fit in with our modern lifestyle. Small pets are fun and entertaining to care for and provide companionship just as much as any dog or cat. Small pets don't need to be walked twice a day and can be left to their own devices whilst their carers are at work; in fact due to the nocturnal (mostly active at night) or crepuscular (mostly active in the morning and evening) nature of many of our small pets, they are often up and about, ready to greet their carer on their return from work or school. As a general rule, small pets require less space than a dog or cat and most can happily live in a flat or apartment (with proper research and preparation) The only exception to this rule would be rabbits, which, whilst making charming house pets, are not ideal for those living in a small space.

Choosing your small pet

There is a myriad of small pets to choose from, with the most popular being covered in this guide. It is really important to think carefully about which species is best for you and your lifestyle. Do you want a cuddly and demanding pet or one that needs less interaction? Also ask yourself how many and of what gender. By ensuring you choose the correct species, number and gender of small pet to start with you are both sure to have a much more fulfilling relationship.

This guide will take you through everything you need to know about rats, hamsters, gerbils, mice, rabbits and guinea pigs. It is worth while visiting a rescue centre or breeder to meet the species of pet you are considering, to make sure you have come to the right decision. No book or help guide can beat hands on experience.

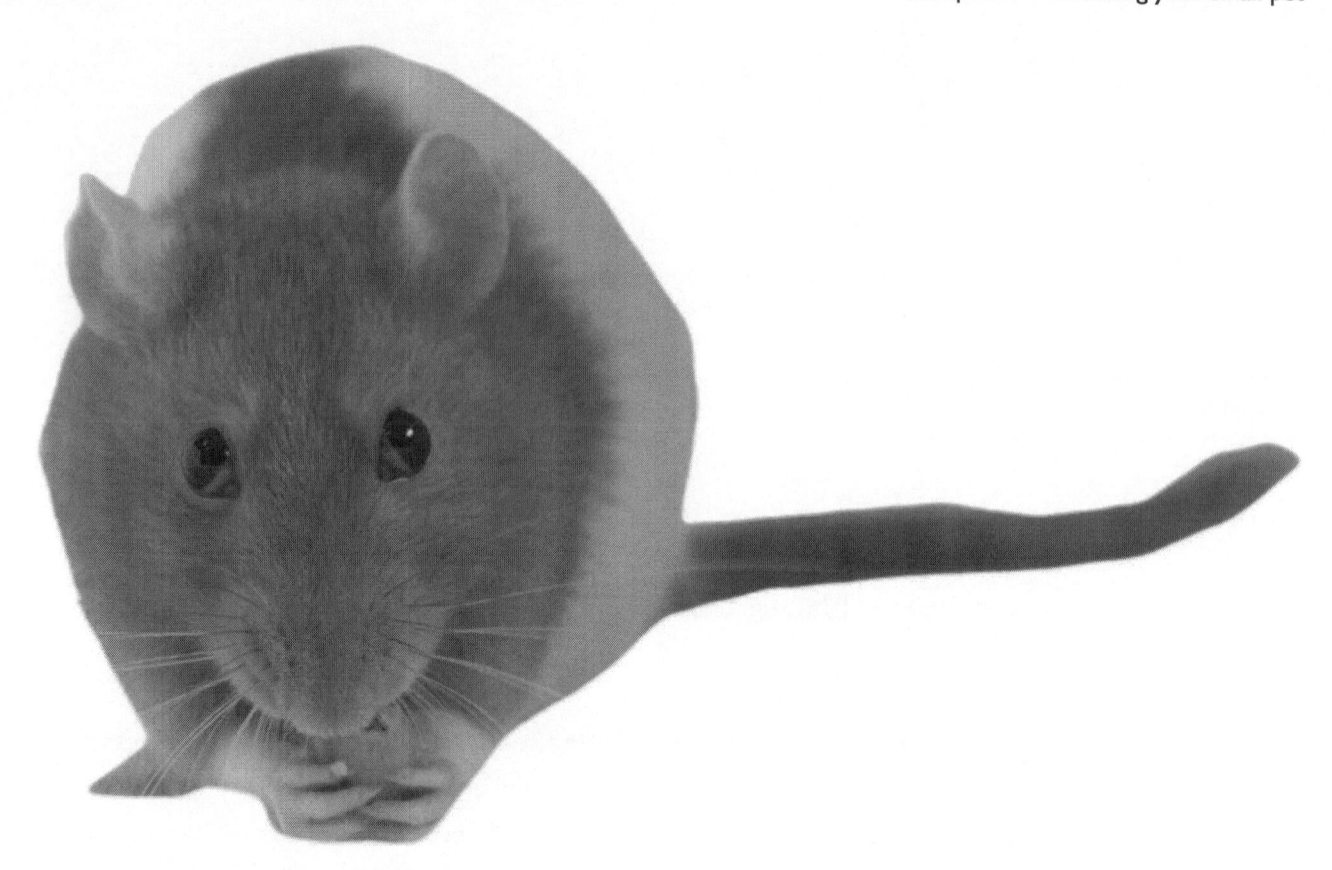

Rats

Rats make wonderful pets, mainly due to their intelligence and sociable nature. Male rats are generally more laid back and lazy than their female counterparts who love to play and explore. Living for two to three years, they form very close bonds with their owners and demand lots of time to play outside their cage environment, they therefore are not suitable for owners who are too busy to allocate time each day to spend with them. Rats are sociable creatures and must be kept in pairs or groups of the same sex. Ideally it is best to obtain siblings, as rats that are raised together generally remain life long friends. If this isn't possible, or if you decide to get a friend for an existing rat, provided you are careful, it is perfectly feasible to pair up rats that have not grown up together. Females are usually easily introduced to other female rats, provided they first meet in an area of neutral territory. Males on the other hand, require more time to get to know each other and must be supervised until you are sure they are happy in each other's company. Occasionally some male rats will simply not accept living with another male rat. In this instance all is not lost; neutering a male rat will allow it to live with a female rat with no risk of pregnancy. Neutering is a very simple operation and carries minimal risk to the rat, four weeks after neutering, once the risk of pregnancy has disappeared, most male rats will happily become friends with their female companions and will be far happier than having to live alone.

Hamsters

Hamsters are very popular pets, mainly because of their undeniable 'cute factor'. They can and do become very tame with regular handling but if they are left to their own devices they can become scared and defensive. A scared hamster can deliver a very painful bite! Sadly they are short lived animals usually living to around two years. The species of hamster you own dictates whether your pet will be happier alone or with company. **Syrian** hamsters must be kept singly otherwise they will fight and cause each other serious injury, **Campbell's** hamsters (often called dwarf or Russian hamsters) and the very similar **Winter White hamster**, generally like to live in pairs, provided they have grown up together. Introducing unrelated individuals can be tricky and is best left to the experts. **Chinese** hamsters are tricky as a recent rise in inbreeding is increasing their tendency to fight with others of their own species. If you take on a pair of Chinese hamsters, be aware that there is a possibility that they may need to be separated in the future. On the flip side, it is unfair to purchase a single Chinese hamster that is happily living with its siblings. Due the fact that Chinese hamsters are so new to the pet market it will be a while before more information is known on this subject.

Gerbils

Gerbils are renowned for being hyper-active little rodents and make fascinating pets to watch going about their business. Living to around three, but up to five, years old they are hardy little critters with a lust for life. With gentle handling they can become very tame indeed, however, their active nature makes them a poor choice for those wanting a cuddly pet. Gerbils need company and ideally should always be kept in same sex pairs or groups. Beware of keeping female gerbils in anything more than pairs as they can suffer from a behavioural problem known as declanning. Declanning is a phenomenon whereby large groups of female gerbils may suddenly fall out and fight. The resulting injuries are often serious. It is likely that this behaviour would serve to help a wild colony to increase its territory as ousted females would move to new territory to begin a new clan. In captivity, however, there is nowhere to run, the stress of which causes small scuffles to become serious. To prevent such a situation, it is better to keep female gerbils in pairs only.

Mice

Mice are adorable little pets but have a major downfall. Even with scrupulous cleaning, they are a little smelly. Male mice have an especially strong odour. They can become very tame indeed and many love to interact with their care-givers. As a rule, mice are sociable creatures and benefit from the company of their own kind. Once again, siblings are best but all is not lost if this is not possible. Female mice are very similar to rats in that they are easy to introduce to other mice provided care is taken and that introductions take place on neutral territory. Male mice are a different kettle of fish and need careful monitoring. Brothers that are brought up together will often cohabit peacefully, provided they are given a large and enriching environment and several water bottles and food bowls. It is, however, all too common that male mice will start to fight and need separating. Previously it has been common-place to allow these male mice to live on their own, but new research and newer, safer anaesthetics mean that neutering these single males so that they may live with a female companion is seen as a much kinder solution than expecting them to live a lonely existence.

Rabbits

Rabbits have long been seen as the ideal pet for children but in fact quite the opposite is true. Although they can become very tame and confiding they require very quiet and respectful handling to become so; something few children are able to give. Their long lifespan usually results in the child becoming bored and the rabbit being neglected. Rabbits must be kept in pairs as they are highly sociable in nature. Although it is possible to keep two brothers or two sisters together, this combination will only succeed if neutering takes place at an early age. Entire males or females kept together will invariably fight in the end. The best combination is a neutered male and neutered female combination. Both rabbits must be neutered for medical and behavioural reasons and careful precautions must be taken to prevent unwanted pregnancies. If you are at all unsure it may be safer to keep your rabbits separated until neutering has taken place. Please speak to your local rabbit rescue who will be able to either help with bonding your rabbits, or will actually have an already bonded and neutered pair looking for a good home.

BEWARE – NEVER BE TEMPTED TO KEEP A RABBIT AND GUINEA PIG TOGETHER. RABBITS CAN EASILY KILL A GUINEA PIG.

Guinea pigs

Guinea pigs are very popular pets due to their gentle temperaments and size. They rarely bite, even when stressed and are a much more suitable pet for children than rabbits. The fact that they do not climb makes them easy to house, they also provide hours of enjoyment if you take the time to design a mini adventure playground for them with tubes and tunnels. Guinea pigs are again sociable in nature and best kept with company of their own kind, preferably in same sex pairs. As a rule, brothers that have been raised together will happily live together, as will sisters also, although males should always be monitored. If this isn't possible, females are far easier to introduce to unrelated animals than males. If you have a single male guinea pig, you should consider having him neutered so that he can be introduced to a female companion.

BEWARE – NEVER BE TEMPTED TO KEEP YOUR GUINEA PIG WITH A RABBIT. RABBITS CAN EASILY KILL A GUINEA PIG.

Vital statistics

	Guinea Pigs	Syrian Hamsters	Chinese Hamsters	Campbell Hamsters	Rats	Mice	Gerbils	Rabbits
Average Litter Size	3-5	5-10 but up to 20	4 - 6	Around 6 but may be more	6 – 24	7 - 12	4 -10	6 to 8
Average weaning age	Can eat solids from birth but not fully weaned for 2 to 3 weeks.	3 weeks	3 weeks	3 weeks	5 weeks	3 weeks	3 -4 weeks	Around 4 to 5 weeks but should stay with mother until 8 weeks
Age of sexual maturity (this can vary with the individual and breed)	Females 4 weeks, males 4 to 5 weeks	5 weeks	5 weeks	5 weeks	4 – 5 weeks	4 – 6 weeks	7 weeks	Around 3 months for males and 4 months for females
Average life span	6-8 years	2 to 2 and ½ years	2 ½ to 3 years	2 years	2- 3 years	18 months – 2 years	2 – 3 years	8 to 10 years if neutered

Where should I buy my pet?

Once you have decided what sort of pet you would like, how many and of which sex, you next must decide where to obtain your pet. Ideally, your first port of call should be your local small animal rescue or RSPCA home. Rescue centres are bursting at the seams with animals looking for new homes and small animals are no exception. In fact, as small animals are so readily and cheaply available in pet shops, the number that are abandoned every year is simply mind blowing. It has been estimated that if pet shops stopped selling animals and all new owners obtained their small pets from rescue centres, it would still take two years for the back log of animals waiting to be rehomed, to be cleared, such is the gravity of the situation. If you don't have a local rescue centre, please check online at some of the many rescue forums available. There are many kind hearted individuals who run small animal rescue schemes from their own homes and out of their own pockets. It is likely that you will find a rescue organisation in your local area, however, don't be put off if they are some distance away and you are unable to travel, the small animal rescue community is very resourceful and transport runs can often be arranged. Many people are put off getting a rescued animal in the mistaken belief that they are likely to be nervous. Rescue centres routinely evaluate the behaviour of their animals to ensure they are suitable for re-homing and often have litters of youngsters looking for new homes. Unlike many pet shops, these babies are always well handled by staff and volunteers and will make super pets.

If you feel you must obtain a certain breed or age of pet and a rescued animal is not feasible, please consider a reputable and well known breeder rather than being tempted to visit a pet shop. A reputable breeder will ask you lots of questions around how you intend to care for your pet and will often, where applicable, only sell their animals in suitable pairs. Having raised their animals from birth they care about their health and well-being and will ensure that they are well handled and tame.

Why should I avoid a pet shop?

Although it is very easy to be tempted by the pleading young faces looking up at you in the pet shop, it is for this exact reason that all genuine animal lovers should avoid purchasing their new pet from a pet shop. The very fact that pet shops sell animals in the way that they do and that they are so readily available is reason enough to avoid them. As already mentioned, there are so many small animals in rescue centres across the country due to the readiness with which they can be purchased in pet shops. Pet shops rely on impulse buys, with some even having special promotions at Easter and Christmas. The animals themselves are often in poor health, having travelled a long distance from the farm in which they were produced. Many of the larger pet super stores are known to obtain their animals from large scale pet farms. Just like the puppy farms that the public find so shocking, so small pets are produced on an enormous scale in barren, cramped environments. On arriving at the pet shop, not only are they stressed, which can weaken their immune systems, but they have often undergone a change of diet, from the one they were fed at the farm to the one they are given at the store. This can have drastic health implications. If you choose to purchase your pet from a pet shop, it is down to you and your conscience to ensure you ask the manager for proof of the source of the animals they are selling.

Whether you choose a rescue centre, breeder or pet shop, it is essential that you observe the living condition the animals are being kept in, if you are at all concerned that the animals are not being cared for, do not buy anything. As tempting as it may be to 'rescue' an animal from this situation, in the end you are simply helping to continue their mal-practice. Also, these animals are likely to have health issues due to this poor husbandry which is likely to leave you with large vet bills and a great deal of heartache.

When you arrive at the premises, it is important to check the following:

- Are all water bottles full and clean? Any green water or algae indicates that hygiene is poor.
- Do the animals have access to food and if necessary (with rabbits and guinea pigs) good quality hay? Some unscrupulous pet shops have been known to underfeed their animals with the intention of causing them to remain small. Smaller animals, in their eyes, are easier to sell.
- Are the animals being fed good quality appropriate food? If the animals are fed the wrong food then this indicates a serious lack of knowledge on the part of staff. Secondly, if the food is of the lowest quality, this could lead to health problems later in life. Remember, young animals need suitable good quality nutrition to give the building blocks for life long health.
- Are the cages clean? Hygiene is paramount when looking after animals; bedding should be fresh, clean and dry.
- Do the premises appear and smell clean? Beware of a pet shop smelling like an air freshener factory, not only are these bad for the health of the animals but what are they trying to hide?
- Are the animals in suitable sized groups? Overcrowding causes stress and disease. Hamsters especially can suffer from terrible stress if left with littermates for too long.
- Are the cages large enough and do they contain enrichment? i.e. are the animals provided with toys? Cage enrichment is essential for physical and mental well being, especially for young animals which are developing their senses and coordination.
- Lastly, are the rescue/pet shop staff or is the breeder helpful and knowledgeable? Do they ask you as many questions as you ask them? The more they appear to love the animals they are parting with the more likely they are to have been caring for them well. Anyone who is willing to sell you a pet with no questions asked is best avoided. Many rescue centres will require a home check as part of the adoption process; this is nothing to be concerned about. In fact this is a useful time to gain advice from some very knowledgeable individuals. If any issues with your housing or set up are noticed, the rescue centre staff will be keen to help you to get things up to scratch so you can give their animals the best life possible.

Once you have decided where you will be getting your pet, how many and of which sex, how do you decide if the animals you would like are suitable and healthy?

Take time to watch your chosen pets carefully from a suitable distance so you do not disturb them; keep a note of the following:
- Are they bright and active? A lethargic animal may be ill. Take into consideration the time of day, especially as some small pets are nocturnal.
- Are they able to move and/or climb easily?
- Are they eating in a suitable fashion?
- Do they appear overly nervous or flighty? A confident individual is best.
- Are they a similar size to their siblings? The runt of the litter may have health problems.
- Do the droppings in the cage appear of a normal size and consistency? Loose droppings may indicate a health problem.
- Are there any animals in the cage or surrounding cage that appear unwell? Sneezing or digestive upsets can be highly contagious and although your animal may appear well, they may well be carrying a disease which may manifest itself at a later date.

Once you are happy that all the above is in order ask if you can hold the animal/s in question. Take note of the animal's reaction to your approach; also take note of the way the breeder/staff member catches the animal as this can indicate not only their level of expertise but also the experiences the animals have had previously. Overly nervous animals may have had little handling as youngsters and may take a long time to become tame.

Now you can look at your chosen pet more closely, take the time to carefully check it for health problems, take your time, be calm and confident and talk to the animal in a soothing voice. This will help you both to relax.
- Are its eyes bright and clear? Any crusting or weeping can indicate disease.
- Does it have crusting or staining around the nose? Again, these animals may be suffering from highly contagious infections.
- Does its coat appear bright and healthy? Any flaking or bald patches can indicate mites or a fungal infection.
- Does the animal appear of the correct weight? If it is thin and underweight it may have been weaned too early, have dental disease or even a metabolic disorder.
- Look at its teeth. Are they overgrown? Do they have any cracks of chips? Rats, mice hamsters and gerbils have yellow enamel (the hard outer covering of the teeth) this is normal and nothing to worry about. Rabbits and guinea pigs, on the other hand, have white enamel. If the teeth are misaligned, the animal may also be suffering the same condition with its molar teeth. These animals are likely to need life long veterinary treatment and/or an operation to remove the teeth. Any animals with signs of dental disease are best avoided.

- Are its feet clean and healthy or do they appear red and inflamed? Sore feet may indicate the animals have been living in dirty conditions. Although the feet can heal easily, the subsequent lung damage from airborne ammonia is likely to be lifelong.
- Are its nails clean and of the correct length? Are there noticeable differences from one foot to the apposing foot? If there are, this may indicate the animal is not using one of its feet readily and may, therefore, have a genetic problem with its bones or joints.
- Is there any staining around its genitals? This may indicate a urine infection.
- Is there any staining or soiling around its rear end? This is likely to be indicative of a digestive upset or poor feeding.
- Check the sex of the animals is correct. If looking at a female pet, ask to check that its cage mates are also female to make sure you don't have an unwanted pregnancy to deal with. Our small pets can become pregnant at a very young age.
- If you are looking at a male animal, check that both testicles have descended – un-descended testicles must be operated on to prevent cancer.

Chapter 2 – Housing your small pet

Ensuring you make a home not a prison

Unlike dogs and cats which have the liberty of the house, our small pets spend the vast majority of their lives within their cages or pens. Even if they are given lots of time to play outside their cage walls, this will still only make up a small percentage of their daily routine. With this in mind, it is essential to ensure that the housing we provide is of the utmost quality. Many pet shops sell starter kits, which in all honesty are cruel and a waste of money. Invariably they are far too small and poor quality. It is far better to invest in a large appropriate cage to begin with which will not need to be upgraded at a later date.

How to house rats, hamsters and mice

Caging for these animals is superficially similar; however, mice and hamsters can live in slightly smaller accommodation than rats. Cages are far better for these animals than tanks as they offer increased ventilation and opportunity for interaction. There are three major considerations when choosing accommodation for your small pet:

- Size – The BIGGER the better! As mentioned previously, your small pet's cage will be its entire world for the vast majority of the time so it is essential that you provide it with ample space to behave in a natural way. As these animals love to climb, be sure to purchase a cage that is both tall as well as wide. A cage that is very tall and thin may be great fun for a young animal but will be totally unsuitable for an older animal that has to make do with a very small area of cage floor. Unless you intend to purchase a new cage for your older pet, it is far more economical to purchase a good 'all round' cage to start with.

A pair of rats require a cage that is at least two and a half feet long, one and a half feet deep and two feet tall.

Hamsters require a cage that is at least two and a half feet long, one and half feet deep and one foot tall. Hamsters must not have a cage that is too tall to prevent them from falling.

Mice require a cage that is at least two and a half feet long, one and half feet deep and two feet tall.

- Access – There are many cages on the market with all kinds of different layouts and sizes however, there are very few that allow easy access to all the areas inside the cage. The location and size of the doors is very important; trying to remove a wiggly pet through a tiny door in the side of the cage is stressful for both pet and owner. Ideally the cage you choose should have a large, centrally located door that allows you to reach every corner with ease. If the doors open outwards, this is far safer. Some cages have hinged tops on them for access, which although very useful, limit the number and types of enrichment activities such as tubes and hammocks that can be hung from the cage top.
- Bars and spacing – These small pets love to climb; with this in mind, the cage you choose should have horizontal bars to make this easier. It will also help when it comes to adding shelving for your pet. Coated metal bars are far easier to keep clean than galvanized metal, as this often becomes stained and rusty and has been linked to Zink poisoning in some pets. Also bear in mind that the space between the cage bars must be small enough to stop your pet escaping. A cage for mice and small hamsters must have a space of less than once centimetre; many a mouse owner has been caught out when buying a cage designed for hamsters.

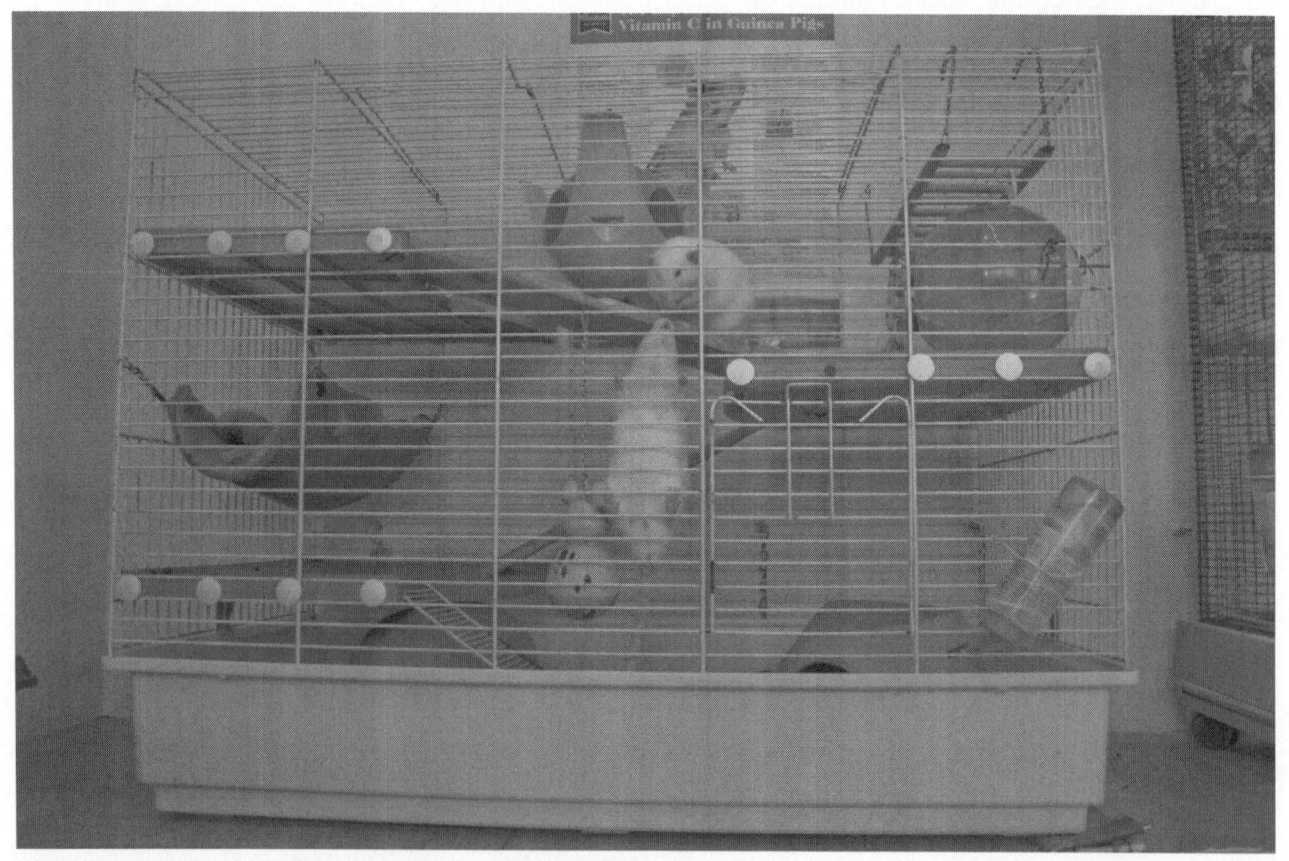

Notice the fact that this cage has horizontal bars. Many of our small pets like to climb; horizontal bars allow them to climb without the risk of falling.

The Big Guide to Small Pets | 15

A WORD OF WARNING, enclosed plastic cages with interconnecting tubes are not recommended. These cages not only have very poor ventilation but in warm weather can become extremely hot.

How to house gerbils

Gerbils should ideally be housed in a large (minimum two and half feet in length and one foot deep) glass tank with a secure mesh lid to keep them in and unwanted visitors out! Water bottles can be attached to the inside of the glass using sticky backed Velcro strips. Attach a long strip of the soft side to the inside wall of the tank on the opposite side to the sleeping area. Attach the hooked Velcro strip onto the bottle and leave both for a few hours to dry. Once dry, you can easily attach the bottle with minimal fuss. A thick layer of bedding must be used to allow for digging. Never use wood shavings of any kind, to prevent the health problems associated with digging through it.

It is possible to make or purchase a wire tank topper to fit on top of a two and a half foot tank. These are great as they make it easier to interact with your pet. Do not be tempted by the plastic tank and wire topper set up available in large pet stores. These are far too small to house any animal happily.

How to house rabbits and guinea pigs

Traditionally, rabbits and guinea pigs have been kept in wooden hutches outside. As time moves on, so our understanding of the emotional and behavioural needs of our small pets has increased. Traditional hutching is very limiting and offers very little opportunity for pets to behave in a natural way. The rise in cheap pet shop hutches can be directly linked to the rise in rabbit behavioural issues. Consider if you will, the reaction you would receive from friends and neighbours if you were to keep a cat in a wooden box in the garden. Chances are you would soon have the RSPCA knocking on your door. It would also be no surprise if the animal in question became stressed and aggressive. The same is true of rabbits and guinea pigs; the fact that hutches have been traditionally used for many years does not mean that they should be used in this day and age.

<u>Should I keep my rabbit or guinea pig inside or outside?</u>

Both rabbits and guinea pigs can be housed inside the house or outside and there are pros and cons with each. If animals are kept inside, the opportunity for interaction is far greater than those kept outdoors; it also stops the weather becoming a factor preventing you from spending time with your pet. Rabbits and guinea pigs need interaction on a daily basis and winter can prove a hard time for them. When it is cold and wet, it can be all too easy to simply provide your pet with food and water and then dash back inside in the warm. When you consider how long the winter period lasts for, it is no exaggeration to state that many thousands of rabbits and guinea pigs lead a boring and unfulfilled existence for almost 50% of their lives! This is, in my mind, unacceptable.

Keeping your pet indoors can provide them with a far more fulfilling way of life and can be hours of fun for you also! Many rabbit and guinea pig owners who bring their pets indoors to live are amazed by the change in their pet's behaviour and personality. Indoor pets often show themselves to be confident individuals with a far greater freedom of self expression than their outdoor cousins. They soon learn, in the case of rabbits especially, to become litter trained and will often leap onto their owners laps (or feet in the case of the guinea pigs – their body shape really isn't that well suited to leaping!) for cuddles.

Keeping rabbits and guinea pigs indoors isn't without its downside. Those that are house-proud should think carefully, as even the cleanest of pets will leave hay and the occasional stray dropping in the most inconvenient of locations. The area in which your pets are allowed to roam must be carefully and methodically 'nibble proofed' especially when it comes to cables and wires. One stray nibble of an electrical wire will invariably mean death for the nibbler! Furniture and wallpaper are also timeless favourites and must be monitored carefully. Extra caution must be taken to ensure that no doors are left open to the outside world to prevent either your pet escaping, or the neighbourhood cat entering! Lastly, caution must be taken at all times not to sit or step on your pet. This may sound obvious, but a great number of small indoor pets are killed ever year by carelessness.

<u>How should I keep my rabbit or guinea pig outdoors?</u>

If you choose to keep your pet outdoors, the ideal set up should consist of a well ventilated wooden shed. Think carefully when choosing where to place your shed to ensure it is in the shade for most of the day, just as you would with any outdoor housing. Some people choose to use a child's wooden play house as these tend to be very attractive with little, ornate windows! Onto the side of the shed, a large run can be attached, ideally this area should be paved and with a fully enclosed wire roof. Although grass may look more attractive, this appeal will be short lived as your pets generally eat and dig it to oblivion, leaving little more than a muddy scrape! By paving the area, you also help to combat disease by being able to disinfect the area regularly, also in the winter, a paved area can still be enjoyed by your pets allowing them to take in the afternoon sun. On the side of the shed, you should attach a lockable cat flap, this way, your pet can choose whether to be inside or out whilst giving you the option of locking them in at night or in very cold or wet weather. This may seem like a very expensive option but in fact, many larger traditional hutches are of a similar price and are usually of such poor build that they need replacing often more than once during your pet's life. A well put together and maintained shed set-up will last for the whole of your pet's life and in fact is likely to still be in good condition once your pets have passed away. Both rabbits and guinea pigs like to chew, so it is recommended that you attach separate sheets of wood to both the inside walls and the outside walls that the animals have contact with. In this way, if these walls become the focus of your animals chewing, they can easily and cheaply be replaced without the shed itself being damaged.

How should I keep my rabbit or guinea pig indoors?

Indoors is a really fun place for your pet to live but even a housetrained pet must have its own secure living quarters. There are many commercial set ups available that offer your pet space to behave naturally. They often have a door in the side that can be opened to allow your pet to hop out. This door however invariably MUST be modified with a little DIY. Firstly, for guinea pigs, the height of the door is usually a little tricky for their little legs to manage so a ramp of some description must be made to make things a little easier. Rabbits however, have a less obvious but far more important problem when it comes to the door of these indoor cages. The cage door is usually made of metal bars with a horizontal arrangement. Although this allows your rabbit to sit by the door looking cute so you will let it out, it also poses a great danger. As your rabbit hops out, or in for that matter, the hind feet can easily slip between the bars. Once between the bars, the design of the foot means the rabbit invariably has difficulty getting its foot out again. Rabbits are not known for their calm and steady nature and generally panic sets in as their prey instincts come in to play. In order to free themselves from their imaginary adversary, they kick and twist wildly and in the blink of an eye, their fragile leg is broken in two. This may sound overly dramatic, but this situation has been repeated time and time again. If you must buy an indoor cage with this door design, please, please take the time to nail some board to the door; also mention the flaw to the retailer so they may pass the warning to others.

Can rabbits and guinea pigs be housetrained?

Rabbits can easily be litter trained and make fantastic house pets. Many house rabbit owners are surprised at how confident their pets become when kept as part of the family.

Rabbits and, to a much lesser extent, guinea pigs, can be housetrained with ease. Both of these animals tend to use one area of their cage for elimination; take note of this area. Once you have discovered your pet's chosen corner, place a litter tray in this area. You may need to secure the tray in place. The easiest method is to hold it in place with two household bricks placed outside the tray, one on each side. Rabbits in particular are renowned for throwing their litter tray around the cage, just for the fun of it! The choice of litter is important, NEVER use clay or mineral based cat litter as if consumed this can prove fatal. In fact, litter is itself not necessary. The best method is to line the tray with a thick layer of newspaper and then add an even thicker layer of hay on top. The hay is the most important part. Both rabbits and guinea pigs appear to enjoy being able to munch whilst going to the toilet, much in the same way as some humans love to read! In the beginning it often proves helpful to add some droppings and soiled bedding to the tray to encourage your pet to build an association with the tray. If you notice your pet using the tray appropriately, be sure to lavish praise upon them, being mindful not to disturb them in the act!

As soon as your pet is happily using the tray inside the cage, you can then start to let them out for short periods of time. If you notice your pet looking agitated or pawing the ground, swiftly, but calmly encourage them home to their tray. In no time at all, your pet will get the idea. Guinea pigs appear to have less bladder control than rabbits and therefore **full** housetraining is rare. Most will try their best though and usually will give plenty of warning before they urinate on your best rug.

<u>What if my rabbit or guinea pig has an accident – should I scold it?</u>

You should never punish your pet for having an accident, simply pop them calmly back into their cage and clean the area with a weak solution of white vinegar and water. Never use normal cleaners or carpet shampoo. These products often contain ammonia which is the basic component of urine. Although the area may smell much nicer to our mere human noses, to our pets, it now stands out as **the** best place to urinate in the house and will be a beacon for further accidents.

<u>The great bedding debate.</u>

The small animal market is laden with all different kinds of bedding to choose from. For the new or novice small animal keeper the choice can be mind blowing. However, the suitability and the effectiveness of the different types of bedding are questionable.

For a start, many claim to have odour neutralising properties. To be frank, this is totally unnecessary and just encourages pet owners to have a poor cleaning routine. Animal noses are far more sensitive to smells than our own, just because the latest, wonder bedding claims to neutralise smells, does not mean your pet is not suffering from the build up of waste and ammonia.

Scented beddings too should also be avoided like the plague. Small animals, as a rule, have poor eyesight and live in a world of scent. Many have scent glands located in various areas which not only serve to mark out territorial boundaries but also help to comfort them and make things smell homely. If your pet is forced to live in a lemon or lavender scented world, you are forcing them to live a stressful existence; not to mention the fact that if they smell strongly to our noses who knows how pungent they must be to their sensitive nostrils.

Wood shavings have long been a topic of hot debate among pet owners, breeders, veterinarians and pet shop owners alike as some people like them and others think they are terrible. I personally believe that **no** pet should be housed on them for many reasons. **Cedar** shavings are dangerous to the health of your pet, *fact*. These shavings emit *aromatic hydrocarbons* or *phenols*; these are the chemicals that make them smell 'woody'. These chemicals have proven in laboratory tests to damage the lungs, causing respiratory problems. More worryingly they have also been shown to damage the liver. Due to the short life of our small pets, the damage to the liver may not show any noticeable effects but due the liver's use in metabolising anaesthetics, any damage it may have can increase the potential risks of any operation your pet may need. Pine shavings emit similar compounds but not a great deal of research has been made as to their side effects. The similarity to cedar, in my mind would be reason enough to avoid this also.

Aspen shavings are safer but still not recommended as the dust levels may be detrimental to your pets breathing. Ask any horse owner and they will tell you that some horses can not be stabled in the vicinity of aspen shavings as it causes sneezing and coughing. Our small pets are the same, although some pets appear to live happily on these shavings the negative implications are too many to ignore. Aside from breathing difficulties, many pets will suffer from sore eyes, noses and feet when housed on aspen shavings due to its abrasive nature. Guinea pigs are especially prone to dry and sore feet when they are made to live on wood shavings.

Of the many kinds of bedding on the market, the safest, and most effective must be chopped cardboard, often used as a stable bedding for horses. Marketed under several brand names, this is readily available online by mail order. It is dust and parasite free, safe, absorbent and perfect for our small animals. It's also great fun to chew! Although it may appear costly, many companies supply this as a large bale, which will last a very long time and actually works out very cost effective. It can also be composted afterward so is great for the environment as well as being a recycled product in itself.

Cardboard makes a fantastic hypoallergenic bedding for all small pets. Some brands come in square chips, as shown here, but others come in smaller flakes.

If you are unable to get hold of cardboard bedding, the next best bet would be paper based small animal bedding, although the dust content can prove a problem for some animals and owners.

Rabbits and guinea pigs must be provided with a thick layer of hay on top of the bedding, especially if living outdoors. Ideally line the cage with a thick layer of newspaper as this will make things much easier when it comes to cleaning out.

At the end of the day, the choice of bedding is a personal one but in my view, if there is even a small risk of health problems from the use of a certain bedding, then the choice is a clear one, especially when safe alternatives are so readily available.

Chapter 3 – Feeding your small pet

You are what you eat!

The old adage, 'you are what you eat' is very true when it comes to the health and longevity of our small pets. It is vitally important that your pet is fed an appropriate good quality diet to ensure it remains happy and healthy. There is a truly mind blowing variety of commercially available pet foods so it is little wonder the average pet owner is unsure which one to choose. Your pet is unable to forage for food as it would in the wild and is dependent on you to provide it with the best quality and the most appropriate food you can to ensure its nutritional needs are met. The food you provide must be of the highest quality and as free of colourants and additives as possible. Many commercial pet foods are stored for long periods of time in unhygienic conditions so do make sure you get your pet's food from a reputable supplier or make your own food using human grade ingredients instead.

In order to know what sort of food is best, we really need to consider the diet our small pets would consume in the wild. Unlike dogs, and to a lesser extent, cats our small pets have remained somewhat unchanged by domestication especially when it comes to their digestive systems and nutritional requirements.

Feeding pet rats

Rats are renowned for eating almost anything! However, they do have very specific nutritional requirements and care must be taken to give them a wholesome diet.

Rats are omnivores, which means they have evolved to eat pretty much anything; however that is not to say they should be fed what ever you like. In fact, a rat's diet should be carefully controlled and modified to be appropriate for its age and lifestyle.

Generic rat mixes are available from all pet shops but as a rule they are simply not suitable to be fed long term due to the fact that rats' nutritional needs change as they age. They also often contain high levels of fat to make them palatable. In order to prevent that fat content from going rancid these mixes generally contain high levels of preservatives. Lastly, many mixes contain highly coloured pieces. It has been known for a long time that colourants are bad for children to consume and that they have been linked with allergies, the same is true of our pets. More recently, extruded biscuit style foods have appeared on the market, most likely inspired by the food used in laboratories across the world. Laboratories are not renowned for their dedication to animal welfare and to the mental health of the animals in their care, and if fed as a sole source of food these biscuits do nothing to aid the natural foraging instincts rats possess.

So what SHOULD I feed my rat?

The best diet for a rat is one with plenty of variety and good quality ingredients. As a general rule the following home made mix is the best bet.
- 30% herbal, non coloured rabbit mix
- 30% human grade, organic, low sugar and salt cereals. Always check the ingredients to ensure no sugar or salt has been added.
- 20% mix of jumbo oats, flaked barley, flaked wheat and sugar free puffed rice
- 10% organic dog kibble (senior variety)
- 10% mix of human grade seeds (hemp/pumpkin/buckwheat/millet/pearl barley/linseed/sesame seed/quinoa)

The above mix can be changed depending on the age of your rat. Young kittens need higher levels of protein than older rats, in fact research has shown that once young rats reach 8 to 9 weeks of age, the protein level should be reduced to protect the kidneys and prevent rats from maturing too early, which has been shown to reduce longevity. Similarly, older rats will invariably have damaged kidneys, due to general wear and tear (an older rat is one of 18 months and above) By reducing the wheat and corn element of the diet and increasing the rice content and maybe adding refined rice noodles, you can help to limit the further degeneration of the kidneys in the long term.

As well as the basic diet it is important to include leafy green vegetables, root vegetables and a small amount of fruit. These should always be fresh and washed thoroughly before being offered to your rats.

Beware of feeding large amounts of broccoli, cauliflower, spinach, kale and parsley to your rats due to the high level of oxalic acid. Oxalic acid is known to prevent calcium from being absorbed into the body's cells by binding to it. This can result in the calcium being deposited in the kidneys and bladder and forming stones. That's not to say you shouldn't feed theses foods, just in moderation.

Orange juice must never be fed to male rats, d-limonene, a chemical found in the skin oil, which gets into the orange juice during squeezing, can cause kidney damage and kidney cancer due to a protein that only male rats have within their kidneys.

The last factor to consider when it comes to feeding your rats is quantity. Research has shown that rats that are fed adlib AFTER they have reached 8 weeks of age, tend to have a lower than average lifespan. This would most likely be due to the fact that food in the wild is hard to come by and our pets are simply not built to have so much food always available. Conversely, underfeeding your rats is both cruel and bad for their health. A happy compromise it seems is to allow your rats to have a couple of hours a day without food, preferably in the evening. This can easily be worked into a routine, especially if you allow your rats to free range in the house. In fact, food can be a handy lure when the time comes for your rats to go back into their cage.

Feeding pet mice

Mice are often mistakenly fed a diet designed for hamsters. Hamster food contains too many high fat nuts and seeds and can make mice unwell.

Mice are very similar to rats in their nutritional needs yet it is all too common for them to be fed a generic hamster diet. Hamster food often contains large quantities of peanuts and sunflower seeds, which although are very tasty, do not lead to long-term health if eaten in large amounts. If you must buy a pet shop mix for your mouse, go for an oat based, additive free rat diet rather than a hamster diet.

It is a far healthier idea to make your own home-made mix; you'll notice that this is very similar to the rat diet mentioned earlier. The only main difference you will notice is an increase in small carbohydrate rich seeds such as millet and an increase in the oat content.

- 20% herbal, non coloured rabbit mix
- 25% human grade, organic, low sugar and salt cereals and pasta. Always check the ingredients to ensure no sugar or salt has been added.
- 25% mix of jumbo oats, flaked barley, flaked wheat and sugar free puffed rice
- 10% organic dog kibble (senior variety)
- 20% mix of human grade seeds (hemp/pumpkin/buckwheat/millet/pearl barley/linseed/sesame seed/quinoa)

When it comes to fruit vegetables, again mice can be fed an extensive list similar to rats, always feed in moderation and ensure all fresh food is washed before giving it to your mice.

If you are unsure if a food is safe for your mouse then please err on the side of caution and don't feed it. Just as with rats, beware of feeding spinach, kale and parsley, broccoli and cauliflower to excess due to its high oxalic acid content which hinders the assimilation of calcium, which over time can be deposited in the kidneys and bladder.

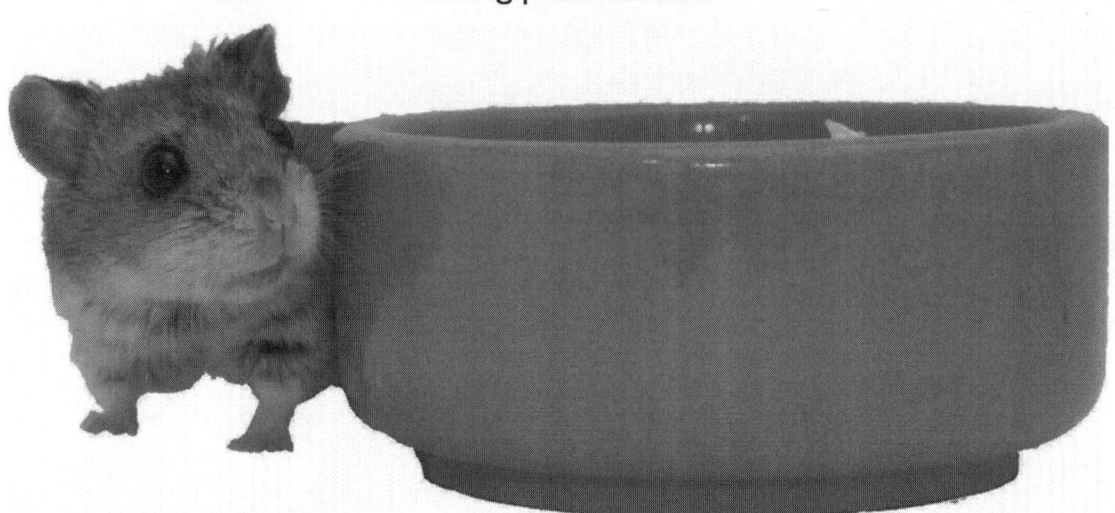

Feeding pet hamsters

Hamsters are surprisingly fussy eaters and it can be tricky to make sure your hamster is eating a balanced diet. Make sure you check your hamster's bed daily for uneaten food before refilling its food bowl

Hamsters have a reputation for loving food as they fill their cheek pouches with gusto. However how much of this food do they actually eat? Modern hamster mixes may appear to be appealing and you will often be pleased to see the food bowl empty in the morning but the truth of the matter will be lying in your hamster's bed! Surprisingly, hamsters can be very fussy when it comes to food and will generally only eat the bits of the mix they find most appealing. As a rule, this will be the high fat peanuts and sunflower seeds. It is all too easy not to notice the uneaten pellets that are lurking in your pet's sleeping quarters when it comes to cleaning out time. Hamsters also have an unusual digestive system as they do not absorb vitamins as readily as other small pets.

Once again, a home made diet is best, however if you must use a commercial mix, choose one that is pellet free and lacking in highly coloured pieces; these are only appealing to our eyes! Once again a home made diet for our hamsters is very similar to the other mixes previously, also has the benefit of being amended to the individual. No two hamsters are alike and one may thrive on a commercial mix whilst its sibling slowly wastes away. A general mix for a hamster should consist of the following:

- 30% rolled oats
- 20% rolled barley
- 10% rolled rye
- 10% rolled what
- 5% buckwheat
- 5% millet
- 5% sunflower seed
- 5% pumpkin seed
- 10% linseed and hemp seed mix
- Organic dog kibble to be given twice a week.
- Soft hay should be provided at ALL times.

It is essential that you monitor your hamster's eating habits to ensure they are consuming everything. Do not be tempted to refill the bowl every day if your hamster has food remaining, instead, feed slightly less. If your hamster appears to be losing weight but is otherwise healthy, increase the seed content, on the other hand if your hamster becomes too chubby, decrease the seed content! Cooked egg can also be given from time to time but ensure any uneaten food is removed as this will easily spoil.

Hamsters should also be given fresh vegetables and fruit in small quantities on a daily basis. It is important for your hamster to be given a varied diet to ensure they do not become deficient in vitamins and minerals.

Feeding pet gerbils

Gerbils should not be fed a generic hamster diet as this often contains a large proportion of peanuts and sunflower seeds. Both of these foods can cause your gerbil health problems if eaten in large quantities.

Gerbils originate from arid areas, just like hamsters and, therefore, are designed to eat a very dry seed and grain based diet. Again, as with mice, traditionally hamster food has been given, but this really is not suitable for their dietary needs. Traditional hamster foods tend to be high in sunflower seeds and therefore are not suitable for gerbils. Gerbils LOVE sunflower seeds and will eat them above everything else. Sunflower seeds are not bad for them if given in moderation; however, they are very high in fat and can lead to obesity. Also, the high protein levels, if fed in excess, can acidify the blood causing osteoporosis. You can find a vast array of gerbil foods on the market but once again, a home made diet is best. The main reason behind this is that different ages and sexes of gerbil have different dietary requirements. Male gerbils, for example, are known for their ability to pile on the pounds! This is bad for their health and is sure to reduce their lifespan. Pregnant or lactating females and young gerbils need higher levels of calories and protein. A commercial mix is simply too inflexible. Gerbils are designed to be able to get every scrap of nutrients from the food they eat and if fed a poor quality diet, may suffer, as they simply are not eating enough food to meet their needs.

The basis for a good quality home made diet is as follows:

- 20% rolled oats
- 20% rolled barley
- 10% rolled rye
- 10% rolled what
- 5% buckwheat or sugar free organic human cereal
- 15% millet
- 5% sunflower seed
- 5% good quality wild bird seed mix
- 10% linseed, pumpkin seed and hemp seed mix
- Hay should be provided at ALL times for extra fibre.

Gerbils will appreciate fruit and vegetables but occasionally take a while to learn to love it! It can be helpful to give this to your gerbils and the same time every day as they soon will learn to try anything new that is added to their cage. Gerbils appreciate routine.

It is important to avoid giving your gerbil dandelion leaves as although they may find them tasty, they can cause kidney damage due to their diuretic properties. Gerbils have very efficient kidneys which are designed to concentrate their urine to prevent water loss and any upset to this balance can make your gerbil unwell.

Feeding pet rabbits

Rabbits are designed to eat grass and therefore must be fed a very high fibre diet. It is vital that rabbits are provided hay to eat at all times.

Rabbits LOVE to eat, this is a fact; however as carers, we must ensure what we feed is the best for them. A rabbit is designed to eat grass first and foremost and this should be the basis of their diet in the form of hay or specially prepared dried grass, straw doesn't have the nutritional value of hay.

Should I feed rabbit pellets or mix?

There is a baffling variety of dried foods available on the market for your rabbit, but some are certainly better than others. They can be separated into three groups, *mixes*, *pellets* and *extruded foods*. Many people are familiar with rabbit mix but not so familiar with its risks and downfalls. Rabbit mixes contain just that, a mix of different ingredients for the rabbit to choose. Although every rabbit is different, most will have a favourite ingredient and one they dislike; this can cause the problem of selective feeding. Rabbit mix is only 'complete' (that is containing all of the required protein, carbohydrate, vitamin and mineral levels) if all the ingredients are eaten at once. When a rabbit has the choice it will often pick and choose the bits it likes best whilst leaving bits it finds less tasty. We as rational human beings can understand we need to eat a balanced diet with some foods we prefer to eat more than others; a rabbit however simply does not understand this concept. Imagine giving a child a plate of chocolate and a plate of boiled cabbage and allowing it to choose which they would like for dinner; I'm sure you can imagine the outcome! Rabbits with their continually growing teeth, need to have the correct levels of calcium and phosphorous to prevent dental problems which makes the issue of diet even more important.

The high cereal content of these mixes can cause digestive upset in rabbits due to their high carbohydrate content. This carbohydrate can not only contribute to obesity but can upset the delicate level of bacteria in the rabbit's gut, causing it a host of troubles, as can having too much protein. Remember, rabbits were designed to eat grass which is generally low in nutrients.

Rabbit mixes also sometimes contain whole seeds such as grain or locust beans which, when swallowed whole, have caused death in some rabbits. The exit of the stomach is smaller than the entrance, these seeds can therefore be swallowed whole with ease but then get stuck resulting in a blockage and eventual death as the hard seed is unable to be digested or leave the stomach via the intestines.

Pellets were originally designed for laboratory and meat rabbits and do provide a more balanced diet than the mixes. However unless they are specifically for pet rabbits, they often contain far too much protein and fat and can act rather like rocket fuel for rabbits! Rabbits fed entirely on an unbalanced pellet risk being obese with all its associated health problems. Obese rabbits are unable to clean themselves properly and can quickly become caked in droppings. This is especially dangerous in hot weather as flies will lay their eggs on the soiled fur. Within hours these eggs can hatch and the resulting maggots will start eating your pet alive!

Extruded foods are a relatively new arrival on the rabbit food market and in my opinion, are the best option to supplement your rabbit's diet. They are extruded, meaning they are rather like a rabbit biscuit. Being designed for pet rabbits means they have been made with your pet's longevity in mind, having a suitable ratio of nutrients. Don't be put off by the fact that they appear boring. Rabbits are grazing animals by nature and do not have the same need for a variety of different ingredients as do other small pets. Extruded foods are as a rule, loved by most rabbits.

Whichever food you choose to use it is important to remember to give your pet free access to hay at all times, I really cannot stress this point enough. Hay provides fibre, both of a digestible and indigestible form, this in turn helps to keep the gut running smoothly, preventing hair balls, feeding the 'good' bacteria in the ceacum (the rabbit version of our appendix), preventing blockages and helping to keep the teeth in trim. I really believe that rabbits should have a diet containing **90-95% hay!**

Extruded foods or pellets do make up an important part of the diet and should not be left out, as a rule of thumb, feed ¼ cup of food per 2 kilograms of your rabbit's weight. As with all animals, metabolism can vary from one rabbit to another, if your rabbit appears to be losing or gaining weight, vary the ration of this food accordingly, and NEVER ration hay.

Lastly, hay provides mental stimulation. Much of a wild rabbit's waking hours would be spent grazing, to obtain sufficient nutrients. An average pet rabbit will eat its daily ration of commercial food in a few minutes. A hay based diet gives your rabbit something to keep it occupied as nature intended, grazing, helping to prevent boredom and its associated behavioural problems.

Feeding young rabbits

Young rabbits, up to 7 months of age, need free access to your chosen pellet or extruded food *AS WELL* as hay as they require the extra nutrients to fuel their growth.

Feeding adolescent rabbits (from 7 months to 1 year old)

From 7 months onward, it is now time to reduce the number of pellets or extruded food you feed your rabbit, whilst continuing to give unlimited access to good quality hay. The amount you feed will depend on your rabbit's size and breed, ideally feed twice a day. As a guide give around ¼ cup of food per kilogram in weight divided between two meals.

Feeding adult rabbits (1 year onwards)

Adult rabbits must be fed a primarily hay and grass based diet with a small amount of extruded food or pellets daily. Feed ¼ cup of food per 2 kilograms of your rabbit's weight. As with all animals, metabolism can vary from one rabbit to another, if your rabbit appears to be losing or gaining weight, vary the ration of this food accordingly, and NEVER ration hay.

Old rabbits (6 years onwards)

Some older rabbits may need to be fed a larger amount of extruded food or pellet than they were when they were younger. If necessary, give free access to as much as they would like, just like when they were babies. If your rabbit is losing weight then it must be checked by a vet.

Vegetables and other tasty treats

We love to spoil our pets, rabbits with their doleful eyes have an ability to melt our hearts, and you can't help but want to make them happy! On visiting any pet shop you are bombarded with a huge variety of different treats for your rabbit with bright packaging telling you how good they are for your pet. Sadly as a rule, they are far from healthy, being more like junk food than a healthy snack, with some being potentially dangerous!

The brightly coloured processed cereal treats or the fruit, nut or popcorn sticks (often held together with sugar and honey) contain high levels of sugar, starch and fat and very little fibre.

As mentioned earlier, the rabbit's delicate digestion relies on bacteria to digest food. Near the end of the intestines is an extra part known as the ceacum, this is similar to our appendix but much, much larger and full of bacteria. These bacteria help to break down the fibre in the grasses eaten. When a rabbit eats a food high in starch and sugar, these enter the caecum and cause chaos. The sugar and starch quickly ferment giving food to the bacteria at an extremely high level. The bacteria multiply and release gasses causing the rabbit to bloat and its intestines to stop moving. Once a rabbit's intestines have stopped moving they can prove very difficult to get going again. Sadly, many rabbits die of this condition (known as gastrointestinal stasis)

Rabbits also appear to have difficulty in metabolising fat often suffering from a condition known as fatty liver disease, this is far more common in rabbits fed a diet rich in seeds.

As you may have guessed, I'm not a fan of processed rabbit treats and believe there's nothing better than a piece of fruit or veg. Fruit should be rationed due to its high level of fructose (a type of sugar) but many types of veg can be given as a healthy treat. The occasional raisin will be welcomed and be extremely useful in training as a reward. I had a fantastic house rabbit that would almost do back flips for a raisin!

It is important to note that kale and spinach should be fed a maximum of once or twice a week as they contain high levels of oxalates, which can accumulate in your rabbit's system.

Rabbits assimilate calcium in a different fashion to people. We tend to only absorb the calcium we need from our diet, whereas a rabbit will absorb most of the calcium it consumes and then excrete the excess in its urine. A diet too high in calcium can cause kidney and bladder stones. Cabbage, kale, broccoli, watercress, chard and endive are all high in calcium and therefore should be fed in moderation.

Grass may also be given or your rabbit and they will enjoy some time in a secure run so that they may graze. Be sure that any grass you provide is free from contamination, whether with chemicals or the urine or droppings of other animals. If grass is picked and given to your pet it must not be left to wilt as fermentation can quickly set in, partially fermented grass is very bad for your pet; for this reason, never give lawn mower cuttings.

Feeding your guinea pig

Guinea pigs LOVE to eat but their diet must be carefully considered. Just like people, guinea pigs are unable to synthesise their own Vitamin C and therefore must be fed a diet rich in this important nutrient.

Guinea pigs can be fed in a very similar way to rabbits with one **very** important exception. Guinea pigs, just like us humans, are unable to produce their own vitamin C and therefore must consume this important vitamin in their diet. Without Vitamin C, they will develop an illness called scurvy and become very ill. Scurvy can manifest itself in the form of hair loss all the way to paralysis! As you want the best for your pet it is important to ensure that the diet you feed your guinea pig is rich in this important nutrient.

Mixed foods contain a wide variety of different ingredients from corn to alfalfa pellets, this can result in your guinea pig picking out the tasty bits that they enjoy, and leaving the not so tasty elements. If it so happens that your guinea pig is avoiding the ingredients that contain the supplemented vitamin C, you will soon have an ill guinea pig on your hands.

In order to counteract this and to prevent selective feeding, there is now a wide variety of pelleted and extruded guinea pig diets on the market to choose from. In this way, your guinea pig will be consuming the vitamins it needs with every mouthful.

It is also important to remember that guinea pigs were designed and built to eat grass and therefore should always have access to good quality hay. Hay not only provides essential dietary fibre, but also helps to counteract boredom. A guinea pig that is fed a diet with insufficient fibre will sometimes be known to eat its cage mate's hair in an attempt to add more roughage to the diet. Once this habit sets in it can become very difficult to break as this 'barbering', as it is known, can become an ingrained behaviour. Prevention is far better than cure in this case.

Guinea pigs must also be given fresh vegetables and greens, which as well as being tasty, can also prove a good source of vitamins and minerals. Needless to say, they should always be washed thoroughly before being fed. Cabbage, broccoli, kale, watermelon, watercress, dandelion , spinach, parsley, strawberries, blueberries, cranberries, carrots, raspberries, apple, pear, apricots, cherries, cauliflower, peach, cucumber, pumpkin, sweet potato, asparagus, tomato, banana, peas and Brussels sprouts can all be fed offered to your guinea pig. Grass may also be given to your guinea pig and they will enjoy some time in a secure run so that it may graze. Be sure that any grass you provide is free from contamination, whether with chemicals or the urine or droppings of other animals. It is perfectly ok to offer your pet handpicked grass but never feed lawn mower cuttings or grass that has been left to wilt. Wilted grass can start to ferment and can make your pet unwell.

Ethoxyquin - the hidden danger in pet food!

A final word of warning. With the advent of the internet, it has become very easy to purchase all sorts of different pet foods from all corners of the globe. With this ease comes the risk of feeding foods which contain harmful ingredients. One of these ingredients is Ethoxyquin. Used as a preservative to prevent fat from going rancid, Ethoxyquin has been linked to various cancers. Always check the ingredients for this preservative and avoid it at all costs. If the food you are feeding simply states "preservatives" but fails to state which one, you must question what they are trying to hide. The pet food manufactures would have us believe that the evidence linking Ethoxyquin to cancer is unfounded as the quantity that was fed to the test animals was greater than that found in their pet foods. Personally, I believe that any risk is too much risk, especially when there are safer alternatives available.

Feeding and weight chart

It can be very useful to keep a food, health and weight diary for your pet in order to monitor any possible health or dietary issues. If your pet is found to be losing or gaining weight, this may be an indication of too much or too little food or a diet too high in treats. It can also indicate a health problem that needs attention from your vet. As mentioned previously, our pets' needs change with age and by monitoring any signs you can be sure your pet is being fed an appropriate diet and is in tip top health.

This chart can be used as a quick and easy way of keeping a check on your pet's vital statistics and will allow you and your vet to monitor any changes or trends. It is also useful to fill in this form if your pet is being given medication, to ensure you remember the correct dosage your vet has advised you and to monitor for any symptoms your pet may have.

Feeding, weight and medication chart

Name:	Species:	Age:	Date:
Weight now:	Weight at last weigh in:	Gained or lost weight?	Date of next check:
Current diet:		Possible changes that may need to be made:	
Medication type:	If on medication what is the dose?	If on medication how often should it be given and for how long?	Any other issues or symptoms to note:

Chapter 4 – Understanding your pet

How to be a true Dr.Dolittle

Wouldn't it be great if our pets could write a phrase book in order to make their language easier to understand? Although this isn't possible, we can learn a lot by carefully studying our pet's behaviour.

As the author Jeff Daly once said "Two monologues do not make a dialogue" never has this phrase had more meaning than it does with our pets. If we are to have a meaningful relationship with our pets we must first learn to understand the messages they are trying to convey.

Our pets each speak their own language and their individual messages will be discussed later, however all share the same two basic forms of communication: vocal communication and body language.

Vocal communication

The majority of our small pets communicate in ultrasound. Ultrasound is sound of 20 KHz or above. Humans can hear sounds of 16 Hz to 20 KHz but rats can hear up to 90 KHz! The majority of rat vocalizations occur between 20 and 50 KHz. The sounds we can hear are just the tip of the iceberg!

You may be surprised to learn that our small pets make a variety of noises in order to communicate with us and with each other. Rats and guinea pigs are well known for their vocal abilities but they are not alone. Unfortunately, much of the message is lost on our ears due the frequency with which it is made. The hearing range of our small pets is well above our own which means we are unable to hear the majority of the sounds they make. Keen to learn more about the lives of our small pets I purchased a bat detector and was amazed at the world of sounds our small pets produce that, until now, I was totally unaware of. I was most amazed by the whistling and singing noises produced by gerbils. When grooming or meeting nose to nose, they produce a beautiful fluting sound, when alarmed, a high, thin alarm call is produced. This will explain the fact that if one set of gerbils becomes alarmed, another set, out of sight will also respond by dashing for cover. In the wild this would serve useful in the network of tunnels or in the thick grass, as a means of warning the whole colony of danger.

Using the bat detector to uncover the hidden world of rat vocalisation has been incredibly amusing, as this high pitched world of sound is directed both at us and at their rat companions. Most notably, it would appear that rats laugh when tickled! When visiting a local rodent rescue I was lucky enough to arrive when the cage of female rats were enjoying some free roaming time. The male rats, which are caged separately for obvious reasons, were all excitedly looking out of their cage and hopping back and forth. The bat detector revealed that the male rats were making a racket at the females in an attempt to get their attention. Sounds ranging from whistles and squeaks to full on trills were being hurled at the passing females. One can equate this noise to the wolf whistle bestowed upon young women as they stroll past a building site! In this case, the female rats were obviously unimpressed by the unruly boys and didn't pay them a blind bit of attention!

Guinea pigs are kind enough to make a lot of their noises at a level that we can hear easily. From whistles, squeaks and rumbles, each has a very distinct and different meaning and will be covered later in this book. Even rabbits are capable of making a range of noises from grunts and growls to screaming and humming sounds.

Body language – a language without words

Our small pets are kind enough to communicate not only verbally but by the movement and positioning of their bodies. This body language conveys just as much, if not more information than the sounds they produce. Canine body language is understood by many but people are often surprised to learn that their smaller pets also use body language to communicate in a similar fashion.

Once again, each animal is an individual with its own quirks and dialects. By spending time observing your pets from a distance, you will build up a picture of the methods and signals they use to communicate. This is especially so if you have more than one pet; you will notice that they are always communicating and exchanging information.

A body language phrase book

What does my rat mean when he…?

Behaviour shown	What does it mean?
Rat grinds its teeth with bulging eyes.	This is known as Bruxing and generally means your rat is happy and content. If you are stroking your rat in a particular place, take note of the area as your rat is really enjoying it! However, if your rat it showing this behaviour without any obvious reason then it can be a sign if illness or fear. Bruxing must always be taken in context.

Rat pushes you or an object away with a front paw.	Rats are very polite animals and would never wish to bite. By pushing you or an object away they are saying in the nicest possible way "Get that thing away from me please!"
Rat it puffed up with hair standing up, possibly swaying its rump from side to side.	Your rat is afraid and is demonstrating that it will bite if necessary. If there is nothing happening to worry your rat then it may be ill.
Rat is puffed up and lashing its tail like a cat.	Your rat is very afraid and in emotional turmoil, it doesn't know if it should run or fight. Occasionally this is seen in very excited rats so must always be taken in context.
Rat flips onto its back, sometimes with a plaintive squeal.	Your rat is scared and is trying to become as small as possible. By exposing its delicate underside it is demonstrating complete submission.
Rat, particularly those with red eyes, sways its head from side to side.	Rats have poor eyesight, particularly those with red eyes. By swaying its head your rat is trying its best to work out what it is looking at and is judging just how far away it is.
Rat stands sideways to another rat and appears to strut, occasionally kicking out with a hind leg.	The rat is trying to demonstrate how big and strong it is in order to intimidate the other rat.
Both rats stand on their hind legs and box at each other with their front paws.	Your rats are working out the social hierarchy without needing to fight. This will often be seen during play between young animals and is nothing to worry about.
One rat pins the other on its back.	The rat that is pinning the other is demonstrating that it is the boss!
Rat frantically rubs itself on objects and digs in its litter.	Your rat if feeling anxious and is trying to reassure itself by making its surroundings smell homely. If a new rat is in the vicinity it may well be trying to mask its scent with its own.

What does my mouse mean when he…?

Behaviour shown	What does it mean?
Mouse lashes its tail at you or another mouse.	Your mouse is very afraid as is unsure if it should run away or attack.
Mouse appears to groom itself excessively.	Mice are clean animals and like to groom themselves. If, however your mouse is grooming itself to excess and is free of parasites or skin problems, then your mouse is suffering from stress or anxiety.
Mouse stands on its hind legs with its front paws held up as if praying.	Your mouse is very scared and defensive.
Mouse licks you or another mouse.	Your mouse is feeling very comfortable - this is a sign of true friendship.
Two mice run and jump around, stopping to groom themselves or each other.	Your mice are having a great time playing with each other!

What does my hamster mean when he…?

Behaviour shown	What does it mean?
Hamster has its ears folded back with its eyes half closed.	Your hamster has just woken up and is still a little sleepy. It would be best to leave your hamster in peace until it has woken fully.
Hamster repeatedly runs around, stops to groom and then runs around once more.	Your hamster is stressed and in a state of turmoil. It would be wise to leave your hamster to calm down.
Hamster stands on its hind legs and reaches up high, often motionless.	Your hamster has heard a strange noise or smelt an unfamiliar smell. It is trying to work out just what it is.

Hamster hisses or screams at you; with some of the smaller hamsters this may sound like an electrical noise.	Your hamster is very scared and is warning you to stay away. If your hamster is usually friendly then it may be injured or in pain.
Hamster stands up tall on its hind legs with its front paws held together as if it is preying.	Your hamster is very scared and acting defensively. You may be bitten if you pick it up.
Hamster gnaws on the cage bars.	Your hamster is bored, bored, bored! Why not make its cage more stimulating? Also ask yourself, is its cage large enough?

What does my gerbil mean when he…?

Behaviour shown	What does it mean?
Gerbil rubs its stomach on the floor or on an object.	Your gerbil is scent marking using a gland on its stomach. Male gerbils scent mark the most but females will do so too. The scent gland is a bare patch of skin on your gerbil's stomach and should always be smooth to the touch. Any lumps or bumps could be cancerous and must be checked by a vet.
Gerbil stamps its hind feet on the floor repeatedly making a drumming noise.	This really has two meanings. If the other gerbils run to cover and begin to stamp also, then your gerbil has had a fright and is warning others of danger. If however, your gerbil is out in the open and all the other gerbils appear to ignore it, then your gerbil is most likely excited or, if female, in a state of sexual arousal.
Gerbil digs in the corner of the tank.	This is a stereotypical behaviour that is very hard to prevent. It stems from the instinctive desire to enlarge the burrow. Some research suggests that gerbils that are raised in a burrow system do not develop this behaviour. Providing your gerbil with more to do, such as safe branches to gnaw on or tubes to run through, can help to curb this behaviour.

Gerbil freezes motionless when held or after cage cleaning appearing almost to be in a trance.	Your gerbil is currently having a seizure or fit; this is common in young gerbils and is often a genetically inherited fault. Most gerbils will grow out of this behaviour. If this happens to your gerbil, it is important that you leave the gerbil in peace and quiet to recover. It often helps to cover the tank with a blanket or towel.
Gerbil slowly closes one eye as if winking.	This is often a sign of pleasure and is usually shown when eating something really tasty or being groomed by a good friend.
One gerbil flips another onto its back and grooms it avidly.	Grooming is a social behaviour and serves to reduce tension and strengthen social bonds.
Same sex mounting (male mounting male and female mounting female)	Same sex mounting is often a way of cementing the social order, with the most dominant individual mounting a lesser animal. Female gerbils often show this behaviour when they are in heat.
Two gerbils stand on their hind legs and box with their front paws.	This is usually a sign of two individuals having a minor tiff and is a safe way to settle arguments.
Two gerbils approach each other and touch noses.	This is a friendly greeting.
Two gerbils stand nose to tail and sniff each other's rear end and genital area.	Gerbils live in a world of scent. By sniffing each other in these regions they not only ensure they recognise each other but are checking each other's sexual status. This is common in female gerbils when they are in season and their hormone levels are altered.

What does my rabbit mean when he…?

Rabbits deserve a whole book of their own, so complex is their behaviour and body language. It is important to note that grooming and being groomed has great social meaning in the rabbit world. As a rule of thumb, those that are in charge (or like to think they are!) are the ones that are groomed by others. These bossy rabbits also have the right to demand grooming from another. Those that do the grooming (both rabbit and human) tend to be lower down the ranking and when a higher ranking rabbit asks to be groomed, they MUST obey. Here is a run down of the most commonly observed behaviours and their meanings.

Behaviour shown	What does it mean?
Rabbit approaches you, places its chin on the floor and stretches its head towards you.	This is request for glooming. If it is ignored, you may receive a nip!
Following the previous behaviour, your rabbit gives you a short, sharp nip.	You have a very insulted rabbit on your hands; it really was not wise to ignore its request for grooming. Shame on you!
Rabbit turns away from you or another rabbit and hops away flicking its hind feet, making an audible whooshing noise.	This is a sign of frustration or offence, usually seen if you have tried to pick your rabbit up when it is not in the mood for it.
Rabbit slowly and deliberately turns its back on you or another rabbit.	This is a sign of annoyance. Your rabbit is making it clear he doesn't want to look at you (you can be sure that it will secretly be watching to see that its actions have been noted!)
Rabbit rubs its chin on yourself or an object.	Rabbits have a scent gland under the chin which they use to claim objects in their territory. If this honour is bestowed on you then you are very lucky!
Rabbit lies down with no feet visible.	This means your rabbit is resting but is ready to run if needed.
Rabbit lies down with its front feet visible.	Your rabbit is a little more relaxed than the previous posture but can still be ready to run if necessary.
Rabbit lies down with its back legs stretched out behind and front legs in front.	Your rabbit is very relaxed and carefree.
Rabbit flops onto its side in a dramatic fashion.	Your rabbit is so comfortable, that it is happy to relax in this vulnerable position
Rabbit wiggles its nose very fast.	Your rabbit is interested in something; depending on the context it may be frightened or excited.

Rabbit suddenly stops wiggling its nose.	Your rabbit is both very scared and about to flee or concentrating very hard. This should always be taken in context, depending on what is happening at the time.
Rabbit is wiggling its nose very slowly.	Your rabbit is content.
Rabbit lowers its ears and turns them sideways.	Your rabbit is feeling a little angry and is warning you to keep away.
Rabbit lowers ears even further and lays them on its back, pointing them backward.	Your rabbit is VERY angry. It would be wise to take a step back, pronto!
Rabbit shakes itself in a jolly manner.	Your rabbit is pleased with the current state of affairs and wants you to know just how happy it is.
Rabbit jumps in the air and appears to jump and twist in a jovial fashion.	Known in the rabbit world as a 'binkie' this is sign of pure joy and happiness.
Rabbit flattens its ears to its body with openings facing outwards, sometimes flattening itself to the ground at the same time.	Your rabbit is scared and is trying to make itself inconspicuous.
Rabbit crawls towards a new object or into a new space.	This is a very bizarre behaviour to witness and is reminiscent of a baby rabbit exploring its nest. This indicates that your rabbit is desperate to investigate this new object or area but is wary.
Rabbit boxes you with its front paws, often grunting at the same time.	This is a defensive behaviour, most usually if you are perceived as invading its territory or personal space.
Rabbit thumps its hind feet on the ground.	This has a double meaning, if your rabbit runs for cover at the same time, and then this is a warning of danger. If your rabbit appears to thump its feet **at** you and makes no attempt to dash for cover then this is a sign he is very unhappy at the last thing you did.
Rabbit makes a high pitched scream.	Your rabbit is terrified and thinks it is going to die. Screaming helps to startle a predator into dropping it.

What does my guinea pig mean when he…?

Guinea pigs are well known for their extrovert behaviour and willingness to communicate both with their fellow guinea pigs and with their human companions. In fact, it is this very ability which has made them the popular pets they have become. However, it is important to understand that although the sounds are quirky and endearing, each has an important message. Not only do guinea pigs produce a whole host of sounds but they also use a range of body postures and movements, both on their own and to back up a sound they are making, rather like the hand gestures we make when talking. With this is mind, it is important to look at both of these elements when considering your guinea pig's body language, or vocalisation, to make sure you get a true picture of what they are saying.

Behaviour shown	What does it mean?
Guinea pig sniffs the nose/bottom/chin/feet etc of another guinea pig.	Even familiar guinea pigs need to check in with their cage mates from time to time. These areas contain special scent glands which tell its cage mates everything they need to know.
Guinea pig rubs its chin on an object or the floor.	Your guinea pig is using its scent gland to mark its territory.
Guinea pig drags its bottom across the floor.	Many people misguidedly think this is sign of worms when in fact your guinea pig is marking its territory with its scent glands.
Guinea pig rubs its hind end up and down on an object as if it has an itch.	Guinea pigs, especially males, use a scent gland in this area to mark out their territories and to claim objects as their own.
Guinea pig puffs its hair out.	Your guinea pig is fearful and is trying to appear big and scary.
Guinea pig yawns when apparently not tired.	Unless all snuggled in bed and genuinely tired, yawning is a sign your guinea pig is feeling uncertain and demonstrating that it does have big teeth.
Guinea pig stamps its hind legs in a rhythmical manner.	This is a sign your guinea pig is feeling concerned about another guinea pig and is trying to appear bigger than it really is.

Guinea pig walks around in an obvious, stiff legged manner, often accompanied with a rumbling noise.	Your guinea pig is having an argument with another guinea pig and should be monitored.
Guinea pig weaves around another guinea pig whilst strutting around in an obvious fashion, with stiff legs whilst rumbling.	This appears similar to an aggressive guinea pig but is actually a mating dance. This is usually seen between a male and female as the male dances around the female, however females that are in season will show this behaviour to other females. Males may show this behaviour to fellow males too.
Same sex mounting (male mounts male or female mounts female)	This is usually a dominant action used by the more bossy guinea pigs to make sure others know who is in charge. Females that are in season occasionally mount other guinea pigs due to their elevated hormone levels; other guinea pigs appear to realise this and do not take this form of mounting as a dominant gesture.
Guinea pig tucks its head right under itself and looks as if it may topple over	Don't worry, your guinea pig isn't going mad, it is simply eating its own droppings! Known as copography, this behaviour is perfectly natural and should never be discouraged. Guinea pig digestion is such that eating food twice allows all nutrients to be absorbed from food that is eaten. Cows and other ruminants achieve this by chewing the cud, guinea pigs, by producing two types of droppings. One set of droppings, known as cecotropes contain only partially digested vegetable matter and B vitamins produced during digestion and are well worth eating again. The second type of droppings are hard and small and contain indigestible plant matter; these are the droppings found in the cage.
Guinea pig dramatically pushes head up when you are stroking it, often with enough force to push your hand away.	Your guinea pig is not happy with what you are doing and is politely saying "Stop it!"
Guinea pig gently nudges your hand whilst sat on your lap.	Generally this is your guinea pig's way of politely telling you to carry on stroking!

Guinea pig licks your hand/arm etc.	Previously it was thought that guinea pig's enjoyed the taste of the salt on you skin but many now believe this to be a sign of affection. Closely bonded guinea pigs will groom each other in the same manner. If your guinea pig licks you then you are very lucky indeed!
Guinea pig panics and runs off when the cage door is opened or when you enter the cage.	This is a natural and instinctive reaction on your guinea pig's part. Guinea pigs are prey animals and nervous by nature.
Guinea pig makes energetic high pitched drawn out rising squeal.	Known as 'wheeking' this is a very common sound and generally is an attention seeking behaviour. Many owners will be deafened by the wheeking of their guinea pigs when they hear the sound of food on its way, as their guinea pigs squeal in anticipation!
Guinea pig makes low purring noise.	Purring can mean one of three things depending on the context and the body language your guinea pig shows at the same time. A low pitched purr along with a very relaxed looking guinea pig is a sign of contentment, especially if you are stroking your guinea pig's favourite spot. On the other hand, a higher pitched purr, accompanied by a stiff body posture can be a sigh of aggravation or annoyance. A sharp quick purr along with your guinea pig standing stock still, is often a sign of fear or uncertainty, usually if your guinea pig hears a strange sound or smells an unusual smell.
Guinea pig chatters its teeth loudly.	This is a sign of upset or aggression; it would be a good idea to see what is upsetting your guinea pig. If your guinea pig is making this noise on its own with seemingly nothing to worry it then a trip to the vet is needed quickly as your pet is in pain!
Guinea pig utters an ear piercing shrieking noise or a very loud, ear piercing scream. This is an unmistakable sound and once heard is never forgotten.	Your guinea pig is terrified or in pain! You must check straight away to see that your guinea pig is ok!

Guinea pig makes a cooing sound to you or a cage mate.	This is a sign of reassurance and usually used from mother to young.

There is one last noise which must be mentioned. In guinea pig circles it is seen as the holy grail of guinea pig sounds.

Guinea pig makes a strange chirping sound; some say it sounds almost bird like with a fluty quality, often uttered with head held high as if in a trance.

This is a very rare sound but once heard is never forgotten, there is much debate over the reasoning behind this noise. Personally I have only heard this sound a few times and then only from male guinea pigs (others have heard this from guinea pigs of both sexes). Some say this is a courtship song, but judging from the reaction of other guinea pigs I believe it is more likely to be a form of alarm call, as those that hear the noise often dash for cover. Many birds use high pitched, thin and drawn out alarm calls as these are hard to locate by ear, meaning the bird can continue to give the alarm to others without advertising itself to the predator. This warbling sound would be very similar and may be a sign of the wild guinea pigs sociable nature. Did they post sentries to look out for danger as meerkats do? Have most guinea pigs lost this behaviour due to domestication? There are still many questions to be asked about this sound and it may be that my interpretation is totally incorrect. However, part of the fun of pet ownership is finding out about your own pets. If you hear this noise in your own guinea pig, get in touch and let me know what you think they were trying to say!

Chapter 5 – Behaviour problems.

What to do if things go wrong

Our small pets can just as easily suffer from behaviour issues as can dogs and cats, many a rabbit or hamster owner for example, will have encountered aggression from their pet at some point. Many people hold the belief that these small pets are either not clever enough to be rehabilitated or, as is more often the case, too small or short lived to be worth the bother trying.

Thousands of small animals end up in rescue centres across the country bringing with them a whole host of behavioural issues. Similarly, the modern, mass breeding of small animals for pet shops, with the lack of stimulation and care provided to the animals they are breeding, is causing behavioural abnormalities to become more and more common place. Although it is said a vast proportion of behavioural traits are genetic, more and more people are beginning to realise that the behaviour of their small pets can be improved given patience and understanding.

In order to understand how to help our small pets behave differently we must first understand how they think and how they perceive the world around them. Firstly, it is important to realise that our small pets have been domesticated for a relatively short length of time, especially when compared to dogs or cats. This means they still retain many of their innate and instinctive behaviours handed down to them over generations which have allowed them to survive in a world where everyone wants to eat them! Being prey animals, a natural tendency towards mistrust has been hardwired in their make up for thousands of years. Being on the menu of many predators in the wild, means curiosity really could kill your pet!

This brings us to the number one barrier to having a happy and content small pet, **FEAR.** Fear is an essential emotion that in the wild would provide our small pets with the means to avoid predators and to ensure they do not take unnecessary risks. It is easy to recognise fear as being the cause of a rabbit running away or a guinea pig cowering in its nest, but many people find it difficult to recognise fear as being a major factor in aggressive behaviour. Aggression in our small pets is caused by a fear of the person, animal or object their aggression is aimed at. This instinctive reaction causes the animal to believe that aggression is their only means of being safe and that they need to do all they can to get that object or being to go away. The growling, biting 'monster' that runs at you when you open the cage, is generally no less scared than the cowering little animal that buries itself in its bedding. Bravado in the animal world is a very useful tool for staying safe if you have no other option, especially when the only alternative is to be eaten!

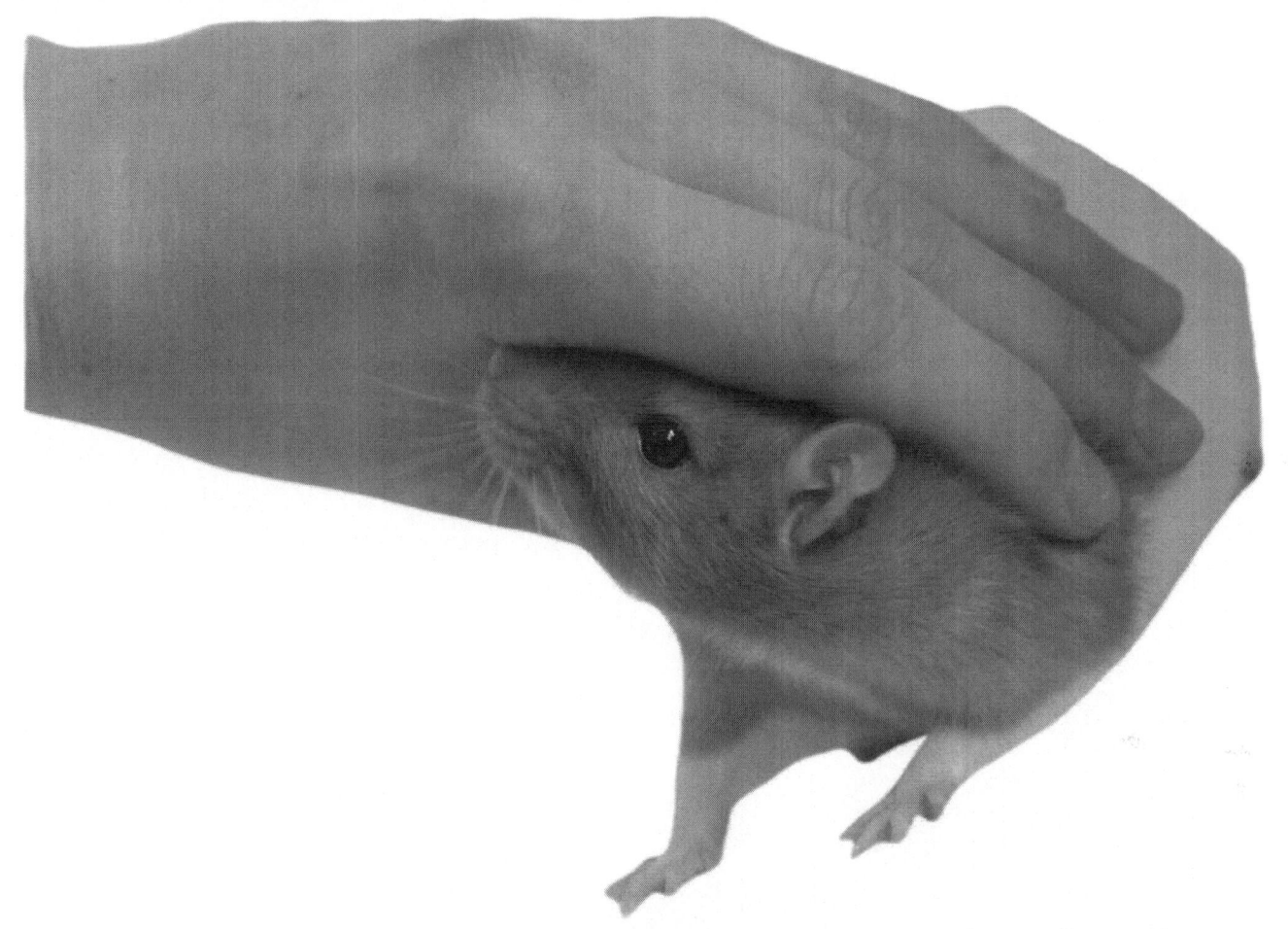

As this photo illustrates, being picked up can be a very scary experience for small pets. Our hands can look huge and menacing from their point of view!

Fortunately for our small pets, we have no intention of eating them, and to a degree they do realise this, however the fear factor can involve many different objects and scenarios, which to us may seem mundane.

For example, let's take a look at the following scenario.

Joey is a male rabbit that was purchased for a young family, as a baby he was a little nervous but the family had little problem scooping him up and taking him out for a cuddle. The family would often have to chase him around the hutch a little but generally had few problems. As Joey grew and became stronger, he became that much harder to pick up, mainly due the fact that he would kick and wriggle when caught. This caused distress to both the family and Joey as they both found the situation painful at times. Joey would often end up with a sore back from his kicking and tender ribs due the fact that his owners would have the hold on very tightly to stop him from getting away. The family would often end up on the sharp end of Joey's claws! As time went by the family became more and more hesitant when it came to picking up Joey, causing him to be left alone for long periods of time. Joey on the other hand became terrified of his owners hands, seeing them as the source of fear and pain. When his owners opened his hutch to feed or clean him, panic would set in and in an attempt to get them to leave him alone; Joey would lash out and attack his owners. Not surprisingly, his owners would beat a hasty retreat, much to Joey's relief. Joey now knew exactly what he needed to do to keep himself safe from being grabbed. Dubbed a 'devil rabbit' Joey was soon taken to a rescue centre as his owners could no longer cope with his aggression.

Here we can see how a fear of something can lead to an animal showing aggression as the primary way of coping with the situation it finds itself in. In reality, unless an animal is concerned about the presence of people or a certain situation, it really has no need to show aggression. Animals always have a reason for the behaviours they show. The confusion arises as each and every animal is an individual and its breeding, experiences and diet, all play a huge part in the way it copes with challenges in life. Even siblings may show behaviour on opposite ends of the scale with one being very timid and the other aggressive. This is the joy of pet ownership, getting to know the way your pet works is all part of the fun!

Preventing behaviour problems. Prevention is better than cure.

When it comes to looking after our small pet's emotional needs it is very true to say prevention is far better than cure if you wish to have a confident and well balanced individual. The latest buzz word in pet psychology is 'socialisation'. Loosely this can be defined as "the process whereby an animal learns how to recognise and interact with the species with which it cohabits" Our small animals need to know how to behave in the company of people and possibly other animals if you are a multi-pet household. Most of the socialisation with their own species occurs whilst with their parents and litter mates, and therefore you must ensure your new pet is not removed from its litter mates too early. The window of socialisation is the time frame in the animal's life when it is most sensitive to such learning and is usually a very short amount of time. Ideally, provided the parents are comfortable enough not to abandon them, all youngsters should be gently handled before they leave the nest. A good breeder or a rescue centre with young will ensure this socialisation window is utilised to good effect. Mass breeders however, tend not to handle their animals at all!

The next buzz word to consider is habituation, the definition being "a decrease in responsiveness upon repeated exposure to a stimulus" in layman's terms, getting used to things and occurrences by seeing, hearing or experiencing them frequently. This is a concept familiar to most knowledgeable dog owners who strive to give their pets the opportunity to experience all manner of situations in order that they become used to them. A lot of habituation occurs without any preparation or thought, for example, many pets become familiar with household noises simply by having exposure to them. Similarly, those pets reared in a busy household environment with exposure to the hustle and bustle of family life, will often be very confident adults provided the children are always supervised and rough handling is prevented.

You must do your best to prevent your pet having any scary or negative experiences. It has been shown that 'bad' experiences are more easily remembered and become hard to overcome. The same is true of people; ask anyone what their favourite school subject was and you may get a vague answer, however ask the same person what their worst subject was who their least favourite teacher was and you'll be sure to get a very definite answer.

Many people, especially those that are kind enough to have rehomed a rescued animal, are not lucky enough to have their pets from a young age, however, it is perfectly possible to give an older pet new experiences to allow it to be more confident in potentially frightening situations. In fact, it is all the more important to ensure adult animals learn to be comfortable in all situations as the likelihood of vet visits and the need to be given medication increases with age.

In order to help our small animals to become confident in a given situation, it is a good idea to artificially set up the situation, but in a positive and controlled manner. By doing so, you can teach your animal to be calm and accepting prior to the situation occurring in real life.

To make sure things go smoothly and to ensure you achieve the outcome you are looking for, you must make sure the following guidelines are followed:

- Your pet's welfare should always be paramount, do not expose them to danger or stress.
- Chunk the situation down into manageable pieces; do not feel the need to rush at your end goal.
- Be happy for small changes and signs of acceptance.
- Try to look at the situation through your pet's eyes and imagine how they perceive things.
- Make the sessions short and end on a positive note.
- Make learning fun for both you and your pet!

Learning exercise: Accepting medication

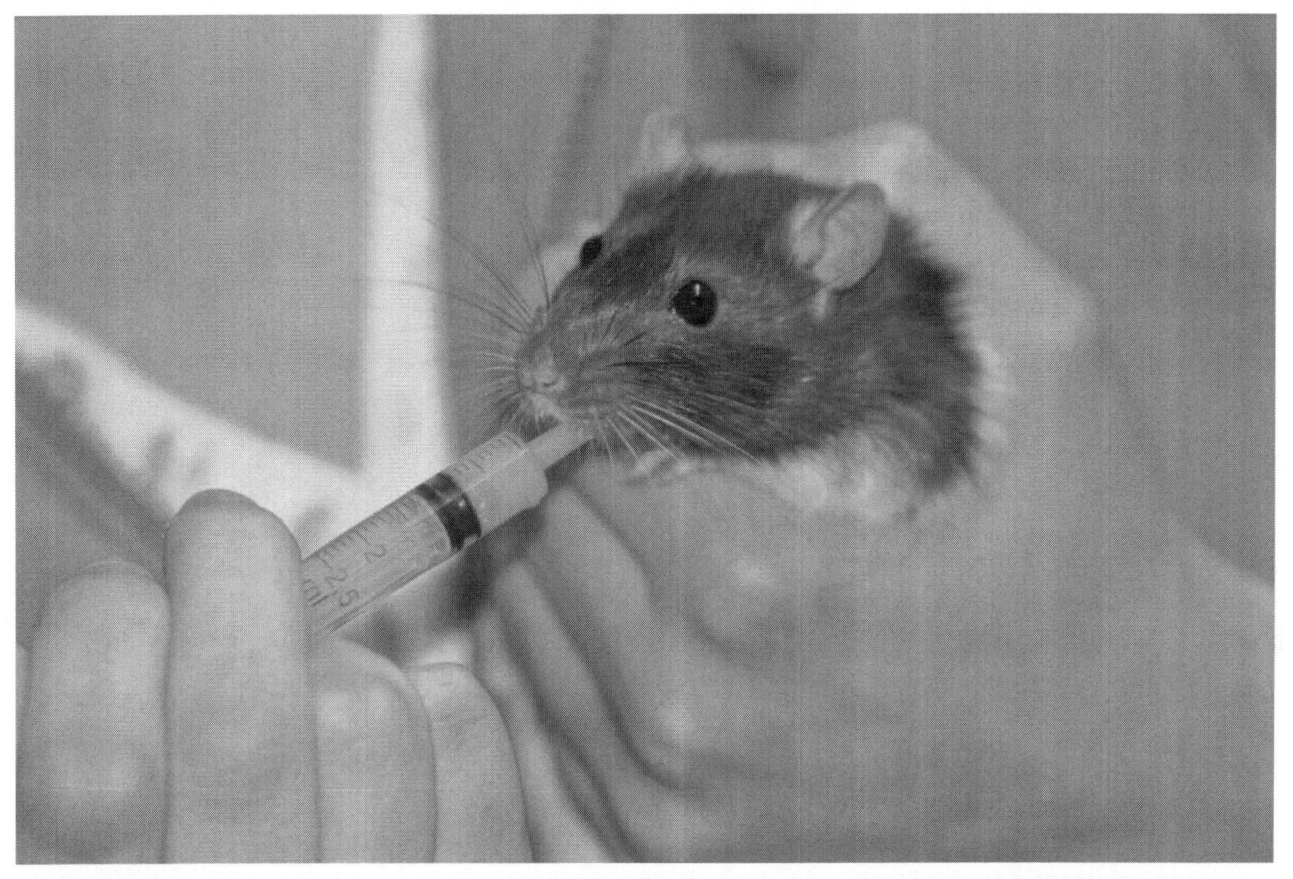

Teaching your small pet to accept medication from a syringe will prove invaluable if your pet becomes ill.

Tools required – Two Syringes and tasty baby food or other liquid treat.

At some point in your small pet's life, there is a high likelihood that they may need to be given oral medication. Rats in particular are very prone to respiratory diseases which can often require long term medication. We can all remember as children how horrid it was being given medicine, as the medicine spoon grew closer and closer, our parents would tell us again and again how tasty it would be, not that we believed them! Actually, the medicine itself was not normally that bad in the end and if it did taste horrid, it usually went away quickly. However, the trauma and stress involved became etched in our minds, so that next time medicine was needed, we had totally forgotten that the medicine was ok and only remembered the dreaded spoon!

This scenario is repeated with pets again and again but can easily be prevented with a little time and thought before medication is needed. Generally, due to their small size, our small pets are given medication orally with a syringe (minus needle of course) The tip of the syringe is popped into the side of the mouth into the dyastema (the gap between the incisors and the first molar teeth) that our small animals use to help prevent them from swallowing material when gnawing. In order for them to be happy when being given medication, it is important that they are taught to accept a syringe being placed in their mouths.

Learning exercise - Day 1

1. Ask your veterinarian for an unopened syringe, without needle and of a suitable size for your pet.
2. With your pet on your lap, allow it to smell the syringe which is placed on your lap also. Do not touch the syringe at all.
3. Offer your pet a little of the treat on your finger, to lick off. Be careful with your pet and be ready to move away in case your pet accidentally mistakes your finger for the food!
4. Once your pet is happy to lick the food from your hand, remove the food, spend a few more minutes with your pet and then end the session.

Learning exercise - Day 2

1. Bring out your pet, and again have the syringe on your lap also. Have a second syringe within reach, filled with the tasty food.
2. Once again, allow your pet to lick a small amount of the tasty food from your finger.
3. Once your pet is happy to do so once more, reach to the filled syringe and squeeze a little of the food onto your finger, close to your pet. Your pet will hopefully begin to lick the food from your finger.
4. Repeat the last step until your pet will happily lick the tasty food from your finger that has been squeezed from the syringe. Once this has been achieved, spend a few more minutes with your pet and end the session.

Learning exercise - Day 3

1. Bring out your pet and start squeezing the food onto your finger and allow your pet to lick it off.
2. Once again, as soon as your pet is happy with this, slowly remove your finger whilst squeezing out the tasty food. If you need to, slowly move the syringe closer to your pet's mouth so that it starts to lick the food directly from the syringe.
3. Continue to offer the syringe of tasty food to your pet, allowing it to lick the food from the end.

Weekly

As with all behaviours, things can be forgotten over long periods of time. The lives of our small animals are so much shorter then ours that a month can feel like a year in comparison. With that in mind, it is a good idea to top up your pet's learning on a regular basis by allowing it some more tasty food from the syringe.

The Big Guide to Small Pets | 57

End result

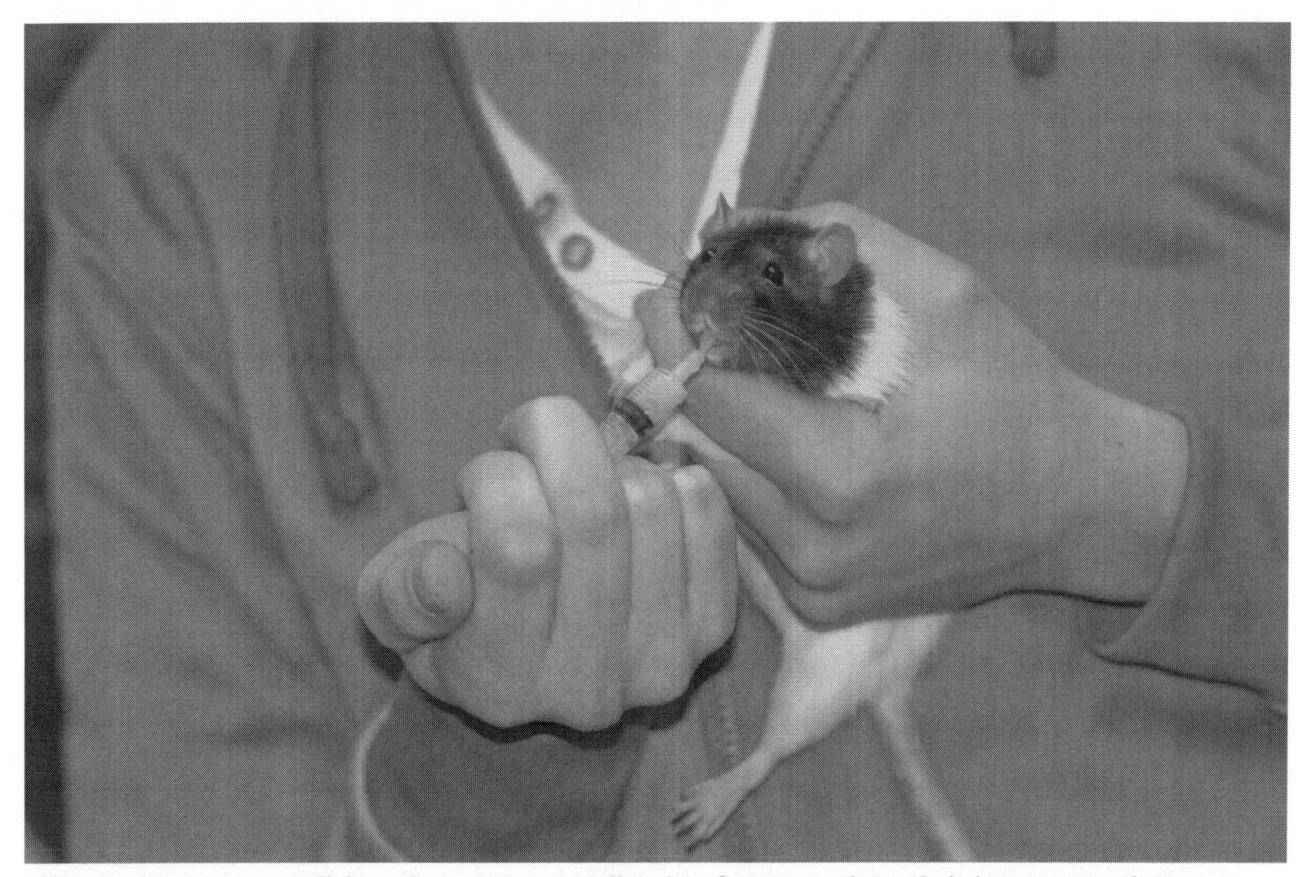

This rat has been conditioned to accept medication from a syringe. It is important that you ensure your pet enjoys these teaching sessions and that you do not rush. It is also useful to top up your pet's learning from time to time to prevent them from forgetting.

After a few patient sessions, your pet will now look forward to seeing the syringe approach. Once medication is actually needed, your pet will not be unduly concerned about the syringe being placed in or near its mouth. When your pet is ill, stress can be a contributory factor to its continued illness and therefore must be kept to a minimum. It is always a good idea to have two syringes when giving medication, one with the medication in and one with tasty food. Firstly give a small amount of the tasty food from the syringe. Then give the dose of medication as required. Quickly give the tasty food once more from the first syringe. Although your pet is likely to be a little confused that its food suddenly tasted horrid, the fact that it tasted normal once again so soon allows them to quickly forget that it happened and to see it as just one of those things. Giving medication will be a stress free experience for you both.

The scary box – or pet carrier as we know it.

A very similar process can be used when it comes to helping your pet to become accustomed to travelling in a carrier. Many animals fear being placed in a carrier or box, especially as their first experience may have been the trip to the pet shop from the breeder. The trauma of being removed from its friends and mother would have been very upsetting, not to mention the fact that the journey may have been lengthy. Secondly, especially with older animals, carriers tend to mean a trip to the vet, which is generally a very stressful experience in itself. Once again, it is important to chunk the situation down into manageable pieces to ensure your pet is able to overcome its fear. In this situation, let's chunk it down and imagine it from the animal's point of view.

1. Carrier approaches
2. Already worried, pet is scooped up and made to enter the scary box.
3. Now inside the box, the only escape route is suddenly closed off as a gargantuan door slams shut!
4. As if to make things even worse, the whole world begins to move as the box is picked up!
5. The box stops again as it is placed in the car but then this awful noise appears and the whole world begins to shake and vibrate. There is also a terrible burning smell! **"Is there a fire?! What can I do to get out?"**
6. The sound stops, phew, but wait the box is moving again!
7. Arriving at the vets, there is suddenly the smell of many strange animals that may want to eat your pet.
8. The box moves again but this time comes to rest on a table, the door opens and a large hand enters the box. **"Am I going to be eaten?!"**
9. The vet pokes and prods the animal and even sticks a needle in it! **"What are they doing to me?! I'm terrified!"**
10. Shoved back into the box, the door slams shut again. **"Oh no! Where am I off to next?"**
11. The carrier makes its way back home again and back to the cage.
12. The door is opened and the terrified animal shoots out! **"Phew! We're home again! I'm NEVER getting in that scary box again!"**

This may seem an overly dramatic take on things but this situation is all too real for our small pets. Luckily for us, our small pets are relatively easy to handle, but try to put a scared cat into a carrier that has never been placed in one and you'll soon realise how true the scenario is! They lash out with every weapon they have and who can blame them? Even though our small pets are unlikely to protest in such a manner it is still important to prepare them for this necessary evil. Remember, stress can make illness worse and lowers your pet's immune system.

Learning exercise – Preparing your pet for travelling in a pet carrier.

Preparing your pet for a trip in a carrier or to help easing the fears of an older pet is actually very simple provided you chunk the situation down.

1. Start by having the OPEN carrier around at all times. Place some comfy bedding or hay in it. Do not place your animal in the carrier yet.
2. Once your pet is happy to be around the carrier, start to add some food inside, preferably something yummy. Allow your pet to investigate and eat the treats without any force, in its own time. After a week or so, once your pet is happy to enter the box, slowly close the door for 30 seconds whilst your pet is eating the treats. Do this calmly and slowly so as not to startle your pet. WITHOUT lifting the carrier, open the door once more and carry on about your business. Repeat this again and again until your pet shows no concern at the door being shut. A few days later, start to increase the length the time the door is left shut until you can happily close it for up to 5 minutes.
3. Again, once your pet is happy with this and shows no concern, gently lift the carrier for 5 seconds and place on the ground. Repeat 3 times and then calmly release your pet.
4. Again, repeat this process but lengthening the time the box is lifted until you can carry the box around the room. Once your pet is happy with this, it is time to introduce the car. Take your pet in its carrier to the car. Give it some treats to nibble on and switch on the engine. After 30 seconds, take the pet back inside and calmly release it. Again, repeat this until your pet shows no concern at the engine being switched, on.
5. Once your pet is happy with this, you can start by driving around the block, and returning home, slowly increasing the length of time the car is moving.

The same concept can be applied to almost any given situation your pet may encounter; nail trimming, grooming, general health checks (teeth etc) trips to the vet, travel to and fro an outdoor run and many others. With both of these scenarios, the key to remember is that force should never be used; the animal must be given the chance to retain some degree of control over the situation.

Take some time to think of any situations your pet may need to encounter in the future and think about how you can prepare them by chunking it down into a fun and positive experience for you both. By preparing your pet for all eventualities, you can be sure that you will end up with a healthier and less stressed pet and you can guarantee your stress levels will be reduced in the long run! A win-win situation for you both!

Chapter 6 – Handling your small pet

A true relationship is based on trust

Our small pets are naturally nervous creatures and it is very important that you learn to handle them in as gentle and as confident a way as possible. Rough and inappropriate handling is one of the most likely causes of being bitten. This is a totally understandable reaction for our pets, as if they believe they are in danger and feel they cannot run away, then they have nothing to lose by attacking with tooth and claw.

When you first start to handle your pet, it is important that this is done at ground level, as nervous pets can jump in fear. Even a seemingly small fall can cause fatal injuries. It is best to place your pet's cage on the floor and handle your pet over a container such as a washing up bowl with a towel inside. The towel will help to cushion your pet's fall and the bowl will help to prevent your pet from escaping.

Hamsters, mice and gerbils can easily be scooped with both hands forming a cup. Nervous or skittish mice and gerbils can be secured by slipping the tail between two fingers at its base. It is important not to grip the tail tightly, but the extra security this affords can make the experience far less stressful for you both. Handling should be a mutually enjoyable experience for both you and your pet and even being scooped can be a little stressful. It is a good idea for you to teach your pet to crawl onto your hands using some tasty treats. Hemp seeds are a great treat to use as most small pets find them irresistible.

Guinea pigs should be gently scooped with two hands, one being placed under the chest and the other being used to support the hind end.

Once you have picked up your pet, it is best to transfer it to your chest where it feels more secure. Most pets will wriggle, not necessarily due to being scared but due to a feeling of instability and vulnerability. By transferring your pet to your chest most feel far safer and less inclined to panic. You could also place them on a cushion on your lap as allowing your pet to have its feet on a solid surface is reassuring.

If you need to handle your pet before it has learned to accept being handled then it is important to make this as stress free as possible. Using a cardboard toilet roll tube, most pets need little encouragement to scuttle inside. Once inside the tube, you can then easily transport them from one location to another. If you need to examine your pet or give them some essential treatment, you can attach a sock to one end of the tube with some holes cut in it. It is likely your small pet will run from the tube into the darkness of the sock, where you can then examine or medicate your pet through the holes cut into the sides.

You can build a larger version of this set up for guinea pigs and rats using a piece of pipe and the sleeve from a jumper or a tea towel sewed on the end of the pipe. Guinea pigs especially are renowned for their nervous nature and any device that reduces the stress of handling can only be a good thing.

Rats can be in handled in much the same way as mice but extra care needs to be taken to avoid being bitten. Although all animals can bite, rats have very large teeth that can inflict a very deep wound. Most rats would never dream of biting and you are far more likely to be bitten by a grumpy hamster than a rat but care should still be taken.

Rabbits require even more careful handling than the animals already covered. Due to their large size and power, the potential for them to injure you and themselves is great. Rabbits are bottom heavy creatures and are known to have a weak point at the base of their spine. This weak area can be easily damaged if your rabbit kicks too violently. Rabbits should only be handled if absolutely necessary as they find handling very stressful. It has been shown that rabbits become far more confident and trusting when all interaction is mindful and as much at ground level as possible. In this way they don't learn to associate people with fear. Life isn't all a bed of roses and there are times when you will need to handle your pet; routine health checks and vaccinations are essential. Using a large towel, cover your pet completely, including its head. Wrap the towel under your pet so that it is enveloped in the towel completely. Pick up the bundle, hold it to your chest securely and transfer it to a firm but soft surface such as a large cushion. You can now medicate or check your pet's health in as stress free a way as possible.

When placing your pet back in its enclosure, keep it wrapped up and place it down, hind feet first. It is important to place them down in this manner in order to minimize any potential for damage to the spine.

Chapter 7 – Clicker training your pet

Big results can come from little pets

Many people are familiar with the concept of clicker training for our canine friends but not many people are aware that rabbits and other small animals can benefit as well.

Clicker training was developed in the early 1970's as a training method for marine mammals. The trainers realised that they would not be able to train whales and dolphins through force as they would simply swim away. They soon realised that if they ignored the wrong behaviours and gave appropriate praise and reward for the behaviours they wanted, the animals would quickly learn to do exactly what they wanted. The most exciting discovery was the fact that the whales and dolphins enjoyed the training sessions immensely and developed a love of learning.

Clicker training is a simple concept for both you and your pet to learn and is one that is sure to have many rewards in the future. Even if your pet has no behavioural issues and lives a fulfilled and stimulated life, clicker training is a useful concept to teach your pet as you never know when it may be needed in the future. As an example, a good friend of mine owned an older rabbit that needed regular urine tests due to medical problems. Fortunately she had spent lots of time using clicker training with him and he was very familiar with the concept. Within a week she had taught her pet to urinate on command, making things so much easier for them both. It also prevented the extra stress that can be caused by the vet having to express his bladder instead.

Clicker training rabbits

As rabbits increase in popularity, so does the understanding of their behavioural needs. It has come to light that rabbits are intelligent animals and as such need lots of stimulation. For those who keep their rabbits indoors, boredom can present itself in the form of destructive and antisocial behaviour.

Although teaching your rabbit to urinate on command would make an amusing party trick, there are many more savoury behaviours you can teach your pet to perform. As long as it is physically possible for your pet and does not risk injury then you can try pretty much anything. The most common behaviours to teach are, sitting, standing, running into an enclosure or carrier, jumping over a pole or through a hoop and nudging a ball.

Rabbits are highly intelligent creatures that crave mental stimulation. Clicker training can fulfil this need as well as helping to develop a bond between rabbit and owner.

Where do I start?

To start clicker training, you need some tasty treats, in small enough pieces to be just one mouthful, and a clicker (you can even use the clicker part of a pen!) The clicking noise made by the clicker or pen is a method of marking the behaviour that you want. In your pet's mind, the click grows to mean "Yes! That's exactly what I want you to do! Well done!"

Your pet does not instinctively know what the clicker means, and therefore before anything else, you must teach it what it represents. This is known by some as 'charging the clicker'.

To begin with, prepare twenty bite sized treats. Click the clicker and feed your pet a treat. Once your pet has finished the treat, give another click and feed it another. Repeat this exercise until all the treats are gone. Whilst teaching your rabbit the meaning of the clicker, it's important to watch out for signs of recognition that they understand that a click means food. This can be as simple as looking at you expectantly, a change in the ear set or with some greedy rabbits, jumping at you like a wild beast in order to get the treat as quickly as they can. If you feel your pet has not learned the meaning of the clicker during the first session then continue with this training until you are sure your pet has got the idea.

At your next session, start as you did previously by giving a treat and a click at the same time. After a few treats, give a click and pause for two seconds and give the treat. Hopefully, your pet will by now associate the click with the treat and upon hearing the click, will look at you expectantly. Don't be tempted to wait too long before giving the treat. Rabbits are not dogs and can become incredibly offended if they feel they are being teased. An offended rabbit will stamp its feet at you or worst still, hop away whilst kicking out its hind feet as if kicking dust in your face.

Once your rabbit has reached this stage and you are confident it knows what the clicker means, you can then move on to putting this into practice.

The next step I call 'teaching your rabbit to love to learn'. Up to now, your rabbit has learned that a click means a tasty treat is on the way, but he simply sees you as a treat dispenser. We now need to teach your rabbit that he needs to do something to get a treat and to persuade him this can be just as fun as eating!

We can all remember how stressful hard exams were and equally how much fun pre school was! Rabbits are just the same. If they are to develop a love of learning, clicker training must be kept fun, and to start with, the behaviours must be very easily achievable.

The first behaviour to teach is known as target training. Take a piece of dowel, some tissue, a square of brightly coloured cloth and an elastic band. Wrap the tissue around the end of the dowel so it forms a small round ball, cover with the brightly coloured cloth and secure with the elastic band. You now have a target stick.

Your aim is to teach your rabbit to touch the cloth end of the target stick with his nose. Start by holding the target stick just in front and slightly to the side of your rabbit's face. The reason you should start to the side is that rabbits have very poor eyesight to the front and behind them. When your rabbit looks at the stick, click and then treat. Repeat this twenty times, moving the target stick to the other side and to the front of your rabbit's face. Every time your pet looks at the clicker, click and treat. In no time at all, your rabbit is likely to touch the stick with its nose. At this point, give your rabbit a treat and from that moment, begin to reward your rabbit only for touching the target stick.

When your rabbit is making an effort to touch the target stick at least 85% of the time, start to move the target stick a little further away. Continue to click and treat until you can move the target stick even further away. If your rabbit starts to appear to forget the behaviour then you have moved too far too quickly. Take a step back and start again. In no time at all, your rabbit will learn to follow the target stick. This is great for moving your pet from one place to another!

Once your rabbit has learned to follow and touch the target stick at least 90% of the time, you can begin to use it to teach other behaviours.

Teaching your rabbit to sit is a fun and rewarding behaviour that can give you both a sense of achievement, Start by raising the target stick upwards, click and treat your rabbit for stretching up to follow the stick. Due to their physical build your rabbit will naturally fall into a sitting position once the target is lifted high enough. Ensure each step is given a click and treat.

Repeat this exercise with the stick until your rabbit is moving into a sitting position with no hesitation on almost every occasion. Then, start to introduce the clue word 'sit'. Each time your rabbit follows the stick into the sitting position, say the word sit in a clear and calm voice as he moves into position. Ensure you still click and treat. In no time at all your rabbit will learn what 'sit' means so you will no longer need to use the target stick.

Many rabbits learn to touch the target stick in a very short space of time. Don't be disheartened if your rabbit takes a while to learn, remember clicker training is supposed to be fun for both you and your pet!

Many people, especially those that have clicker trained dogs, will find it awful that a treat is used throughout the process and that the treat has not been phased out and replaced with a stroke or affection. Rabbits are not dogs and as such, most have very different motivational factors than our canine friends. As much as they love to learn, they need a reason to. How many people choose to go to work for free? Rabbits are more like people that dogs. They love a challenge but most will not work hard if the reward at the end is not worth their while.

The principles of clicker training can be used for any situation your rabbit is physically capable of. These can be both practical and just for fun but all help to develop a deep bond and rapport between you and your pet. I encourage all rabbit owners to teach their pet to run to its hutch on command as a safety measure and to be rewarded for eating from hand also. Rabbits are prone to digestive problems and can stop eating. A well trained rabbit will often be tempted to eat even when not hungry. This can be a lifesaver! Clicker training can prove an invaluable way of teaching your rabbit to accept medical examinations and routine nail trimming and grooming.

There are also lots of fun uses for clicker training, from teaching your rabbit to play fetch, to jumping an obstacle in a rabbit agility course. The possibilities are endless, just remember to make sure you both stay safe and that everything is kept as much fun as possible.

Clicker training rats and other small pets

Rats are renowned for their intelligence. This intelligence has led them to be used in behavioural studies in laboratories for many years. Pet rats can be taught to perform all manner of tricks which helps to keep them stimulated.

Clicker training is not just reserved for rabbits as all small animals can be clicker trained to some extent. The key is finding the right reward for each pet. The principle of clicker training our smaller pets is just the same as for rabbits as out lined earlier however, one of the major hurdles is the way in which most of these smaller animals use their paws to hold the food they are eating. It can be very easy for your pet to become confused as they can forget the behaviour they were originally performing once they are given the treat to eat.

An easy way to combat this is to use a treat that can be easily licked, such as cream cheese. In this way, your pet gets a quick lick of tasty cheese and does not need to change its position in order to eat it.

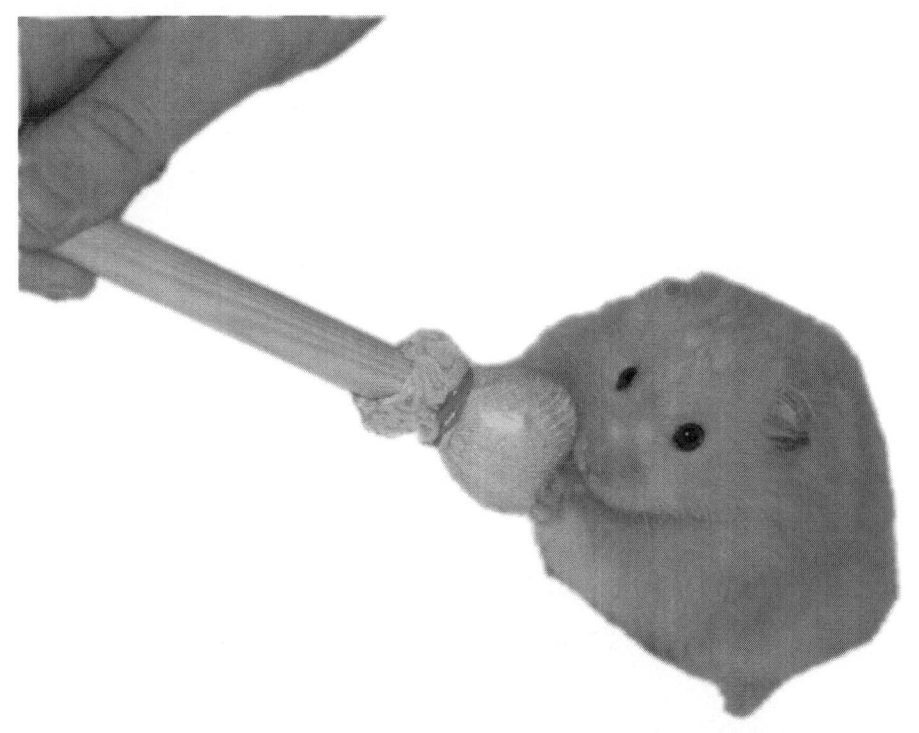

Even hamsters and mice can enjoy clicker training. You may need to experiment with different types of treats to ensure you find one your pet values enough to work for.

The second hurdle to overcome is the loudness of the click. Many small pets can be very wary of the click the clicker produces. There are some great clickers on the market that allow the volume of the click to be reduced. If you are unable to get your hands on one of these, then the click of a pen can be a good substitute. You may also like try wrapping the clicker in piece of cloth or towel to dull the sound.

Some pets may find the volume of a conventional clicker a little unnerving. You may wish to use a pen or to wrap the clicker in a towel instead.

Chapter 8 – Getting in TTouch with your small pet

Encouraging harmony, cooperation and trust between humans and animals

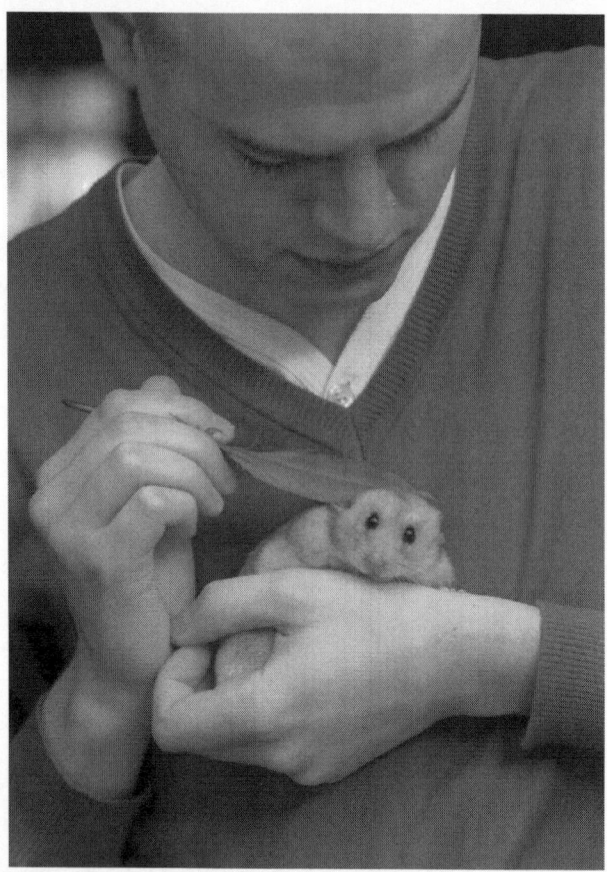

The Tellington TTouch technique not only helps to overcome a wide range of behaviour issues with small pets but also allows a relationship based on trust and understanding to develop. Many small animal owners comment that they developed a stronger bond with their pets since using the TTouch exercises.

Earlier in this book we looked at exercises to prepare a young animal for its life ahead but what should you do to help an older animal with behaviour issues?

Older animals, especially those that have come from neglectful pasts, may have a wide range of behavioural issues, ranging from nervousness to aggression. Traditional training methods as used for dogs and cats are hard to employ with our small friends namely due to their prey animal instincts. Many people with nervous or aggressive small pets attempt to overcome these problems by forcing their pet to be held, in the notion that it will soon get used to it. This really is not an acceptable method of helping any animal to overcome its fears. Similar to a process known as 'flooding', forcing your small pet to be held simply produces an animal that is too scared and shut down emotionally to put up a fight. Many animals respond to this technique by becoming even more scared and trying twice as hard to escape or attack in the future.

In order to help our pets to be as confident and content as possible it is important to use a technique based on communication and kindness. This is where the Tellington TTouch technique steps in.

What is TTouch?

The Tellington TTouch technique or TTouch as it is known, is a method of helping animals of all species, to become more confident, balanced, calm and controlled, whilst learning to behave in a more mindful manner. A combination of circular movements of the fingers and hands all over the body help to release tension and increase body awareness. This in turn helps to build a deep rapport between animals and their human companions and promotes a feeling of mutual trust and understanding.

Isn't this massage?

No, the TTouch works on a cellular level and works with the central nervous system, rather than working with muscle groups as happens with massage. Linda Tellington-Jones, the founder of TTouch describes this as "a little like turning on the electric lights of the body" The TTouch body work is a very light and gentle movement.

How does it work?

The Tellington TTouch has an effect on so many different levels. In order to understand how the TTouch works we first need to understand a phenomenon known as tension patterns and also how an animal's posture affects its behaviour.

The way in which an animal or person holds its body is known as its posture. Many of us can recall as children being told by our parents to "stand up straight", this was normally because we were slouching and therefore were deemed to have a bad posture. Equally you can probably remember how hard it was to consciously attempt to change your posture, as slouching was something you simply did naturally as this posture had become habitual.

As adults, especially if working at a computer all day, we often arrive home with a painful back and shoulders due to the unnatural posture we are made to assume whilst at work.

Now imagine how this bad posture makes you feel. Even if you are not physically in pain, you are likely to arrive home feeling grumpy and irritable. When voicing your annoyance to friends or family, it is common to be told to "keep your chin up" Without thinking about it, we all subconsciously change the way we hold our bodies; straightening our backs and lifting our heads. Surprisingly this makes us feel slightly better. Simply by changing our body posture we have made ourselves feel far happier. The way we use our bodies directly affects the way we think and feel; the same is true of our small pets. The way in which they use their bodies effects their emotions, their ability to learn, their confidence and their ability to adapt and change their behaviour.

What causes bad posture?

The skin, bones, muscles and ligaments of ourselves and our small pets are held together with tension. Without tension, we would all simply be a big blob of body parts without the ability to move. Tension is essential for life. Our bodies are ever changing, learning to tense and relax in relation to the task in hand but there are a myriad of different circumstances and events that cause unwanted tension patterns to occur. Tension patterns are areas of tension that can occur in any number of different areas throughout the body. These tense areas can inhibit movement, sometimes on a minuscule level. This tension affects the animal's posture which in turn affects its emotional state. Tension patterns can occur for many reasons, both on a physical and mental level. Emotional trauma, for example can set up tension patterns, which actually can result in a vicious circle being created as trauma creates tension which creates more trauma, which creates more tension... you can see where I'm going with this. There are many physical causes of tension patterns, starting with the most physically demanding of events, birth. Birth is very stressful for the body and causes many animals and people to be born with tension patterns. Young animals that are learning to use their new and growing bodies often develop tension patterns through jumping and twisting or playing roughly with their siblings. Adult animals, too, can easily suffer if they have a fall or a knock. Lastly, as animals approach their senior years, ageing muscles and joints and a decrease in general mobility mean the body has to be moved in a totally new way. This again causes many tension patters to develop.

How can TTouch help?

TTouch helps an animal to release these areas of tension by increasing the body's self awareness and helping the animal to become more balanced and integrated. As the body is made more aware of the tension patterns it is holding, and once it is shown an alternative, these areas of tension rapidly reduce. As the tension diminishes, so does the inappropriate behaviour the animal may be demonstrating as they reach a level of physical and emotional balance. Similarly, circulation is increased which helps to reduce stiffness and aid healing.

The aaah factor

The TTouch technique is very relaxing for both the animal and the person giving the TTouch as a myriad of 'happy hormones' are released into the blood stream. These include the chemical Dopamine which causes the animal to feel great. These happy hormones help to change an animal's perception of human contact as they soon realise it feels goooooood!

It's all in the mind

The TTouch also has a profound effect on the brain of our pets. Whilst being TTouched, studies have shown a combination of brain waves is created which brings our pets into what is known as an *awakened mind state*. In a nutshell this means the brain of our pets is open to learning new experiences and the instinct to run away or attack is diminished. This fight or flight instinct is hard wired into our small pets make up, by helping our pets to overcome this instinct, the possibilities for change are amazing. It also provides a link between the conscious and unconscious brain allowing deep set fears and phobias to be overcome. The brain of our small pets can easily become shut down with fear and stress, the ability to bring them into this awakened mind state is invaluable in speeding up the process of helping them to become confident and balanced individuals.

Another key to the success of TTouch is the fact that the movements are non-habitual, i.e. different from anything the animal will usually experience. When the brain experiences something new, it kicks into action and becomes aware of everything around it. Think how it feels when you get a stone in your shoe; usually you are able to walk happily without even noticing your feet. Your subconscious brain does all the work. As soon as you have a stone in your shoe, everything changes and you are now **SO** aware of your foot that you can think of nothing **BUT** your foot and walking becomes tricky. The stony culprit usually turns out to be very tiny, so it isn't the stone itself that is causing you to have a problem walking. The difficulty is caused by the new and increased awareness you now have of your own foot causing you to feel unbalanced. Now the TTouch technique does not employ stones, but this example does demonstrate how a small and seemingly insignificant sensation, provided it is non-habitual, can bring about heightened awareness of our bodies and surroundings. Once our small pets are aware of the way they use their bodies, they quickly learn new and more appropriate ways of doing so, therefore becoming more physically balanced. As this balance is achieved so many behavioural problems simply disappear.

Learning exercise – how aware are you?

A fun and simple exercise to try: Without looking and with as little thought as possible, cross your arms in the opposite way than you would normally do so. Many people find this tricky as there arms simply 'want' to cross in the usual fashion. Once they are crossed, sit a while and feel just how aware you are of your arms and upper body. Can you feel the position of your shoulders? Does your neck feel relaxed or tense? Do you feel you have to consciously keep your back straight? By crossing your arms wrongly, your brain is woken by the unusual sensation and soon takes note of everything it can feel.

Observation

So far, we have discovered that the way an animal uses its body affects the way it thinks and behaves. We have also found out that TTouch can help to address the problem and produce a well balanced individual. With this in mind, it is all too easy to be tempted to jump on in and start to use the TTouch techniques right away. However, before you do, it is important to take time to observe your pet to see how it uses its body before you start. Knowing the way your pet is holding its body and the tension it currently has not only allows you to notice changes AFTER you have given some TTouch but experience shows that particular areas of tension are linked to particular behaviours or fears. Animals that have tension in the hindquarters and tail (if they have one!) will often be afraid of loud or unfamiliar noises. Those that are tense in the head and neck area will often bite without warning as they tend to be very reactive to movement.

What should I look out for?

Observing your pet's posture can be tricky as it can be hard to notice things that your pet regularly does. Take your time to watch your pet. How does your pet walk? Does it walk smoothly and evenly? Or does it appear to walk stiffly or hop? Does it walk daintily on its toes or appear very flat footed? When your pet is resting, does it appear relaxed and able to lie down comfortably or does it appear tense and hunched? Can it bend freely when climbing or jumping?

Hands on

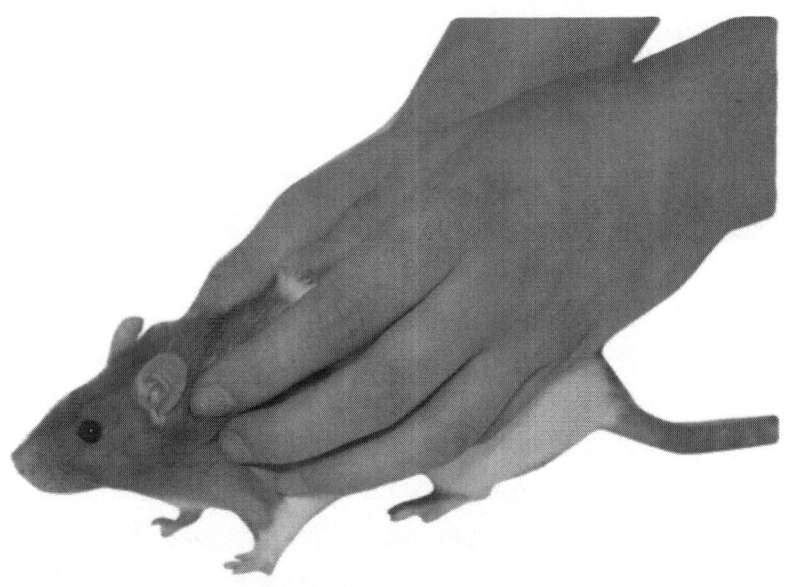

It is important to remain calm and mindful when feeling your pet's body for areas of tension. Try not to be too clinical in your approach as your pet may find this unnerving.

Next, if your pet will allow, use your hands to gently feel for any areas of tension in your pet's body. These will feel like tight and sometimes overly warm or cold areas and the skin may not move as freely. Your pet may be unhappy at you touching a certain area and may react by wriggling or biting.

Do you notice any waves or spasms of your pet's skin as you touch it? This is a sure sign that this area is holding tension.

Look at your pet's coat; are there any areas that appear dull and lifeless? Does the hair point in a different direction? Areas of tension cause the hair to be pulled upwards as the tense skin is pulled taut, this in turn means less light reflects from the hair shaft, the hair itself therefore appears dull as there is no shine. The texture of the hair may be course, flaky and dry due to a lack of the conditioning oil the coat requires, tension in the body inhibits oil production. Some black animals may show a totally different coat colour with tense areas appearing as a dull brown rather than a rich, shiny black.

Remember to be honest when you are observing your pet and note that it is not a case of picking faults in your pet. Every animal will have areas of tension and it is not a judgment that we are making when we take note of these issues. The better you get to know the ins and outs of your pet, the better able you will be to help them become well balanced.

What are the TTouches?

There is a wide variety of different TTouches to choose from and each has a different name. Linda Tellington-Jones, the founder of TTouch, named each one after the animal that inspired the Touch or the animal that the Touch reminded her of. The names may seem strange, but by naming them in this way, the TTouches are far easier to learn than if they were simply named TTouch 1, 2, 3 etc. It is this beautiful simplicity that has enabled the TTouch technique to be learned by thousands of people across the world, including children.

The three types

Of the many TTouches that we can offer our small pets, most can be grouped into one of the following categories; Circular TTouches, Lifting TTouches and Sliding TTouches.

Circular TTouches

The circular TTouches form the foundation for the majority of the TTouches we offer our small companions. They are based around a one and a quarter movement of the animal's skin, usually using the fingers or hands. The very same TTouches are used on animals of all sizes, just on various different scales. Many people ask why we use a one and quarter circle; at this moment in time, we simply do not have an answer. The one and quarter circle has proven time and time again to be more effective and pleasurable than any other smaller or larger combination. As the TTouch has branched into being used for people, (known as TTouch for You) we have been lucky enough to receive feedback from hundreds of people, who have also confirmed the same.

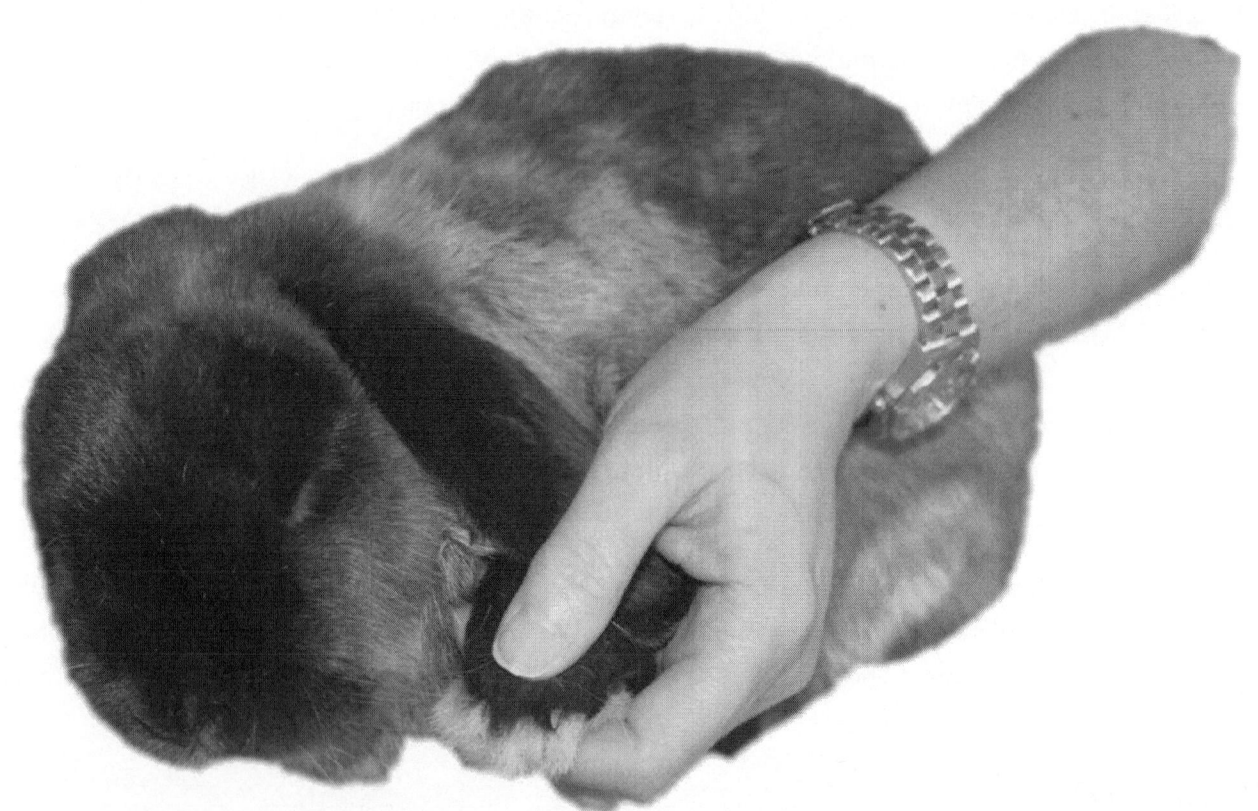

The circular TTouches can be performed on any area of your pet's body. This rabbit is enjoying TTouch on its feet in order to prepare it for having its nails trimmed.

Lifting TTouches

The main lifting TTouch that we will use for our small pets is known as the Python Lift. Lifting TTouches are great for easing tension in very tight areas and are very effective for our little pets. The aim is to lift the skin and underlying muscle by a tiny fraction, pause for a few seconds and then slowly release the area back down once more. One of the theories behind the effectiveness of the lifting movement is that the first lift causes MORE tension to start with. The pause gives the body time to realise the tension is being held in your hand. The **long** and **slow** release appears to trick the body into not only releasing the tension that you have just created, but also to release the tension that was present before.

Sliding TTouches

There are many sliding TTouches to choose from, the most important being Noah's March. You may think a sliding TTouch is simply the same as stroking your pet, but there is a fundamental difference that sets the sliding TTouches apart. When giving a sliding TTouch, it is important to use a slow, steady, even pressure and to be mindful and focused. Feel the contours of your pet's body beneath your hand and visualise a connection to you pet, be sure to breathe and remain relaxed. Sliding TTouches are great for helping your pet to become fully connected from top to tail. They are always used at the start and end of a session.

The TTouches

As we mentioned earlier, many of the TTouches are based on a circular movement of your pet's skin, and it is these that we shall look at first of all.

The Clouded Leopard TTouch is the basic circular TTouch that many of the other TTouches evolved from. You can use this TTouch on any part of your pet's body, provided they are happy for you to do so.

How to do the Clouded Leopard TTouch

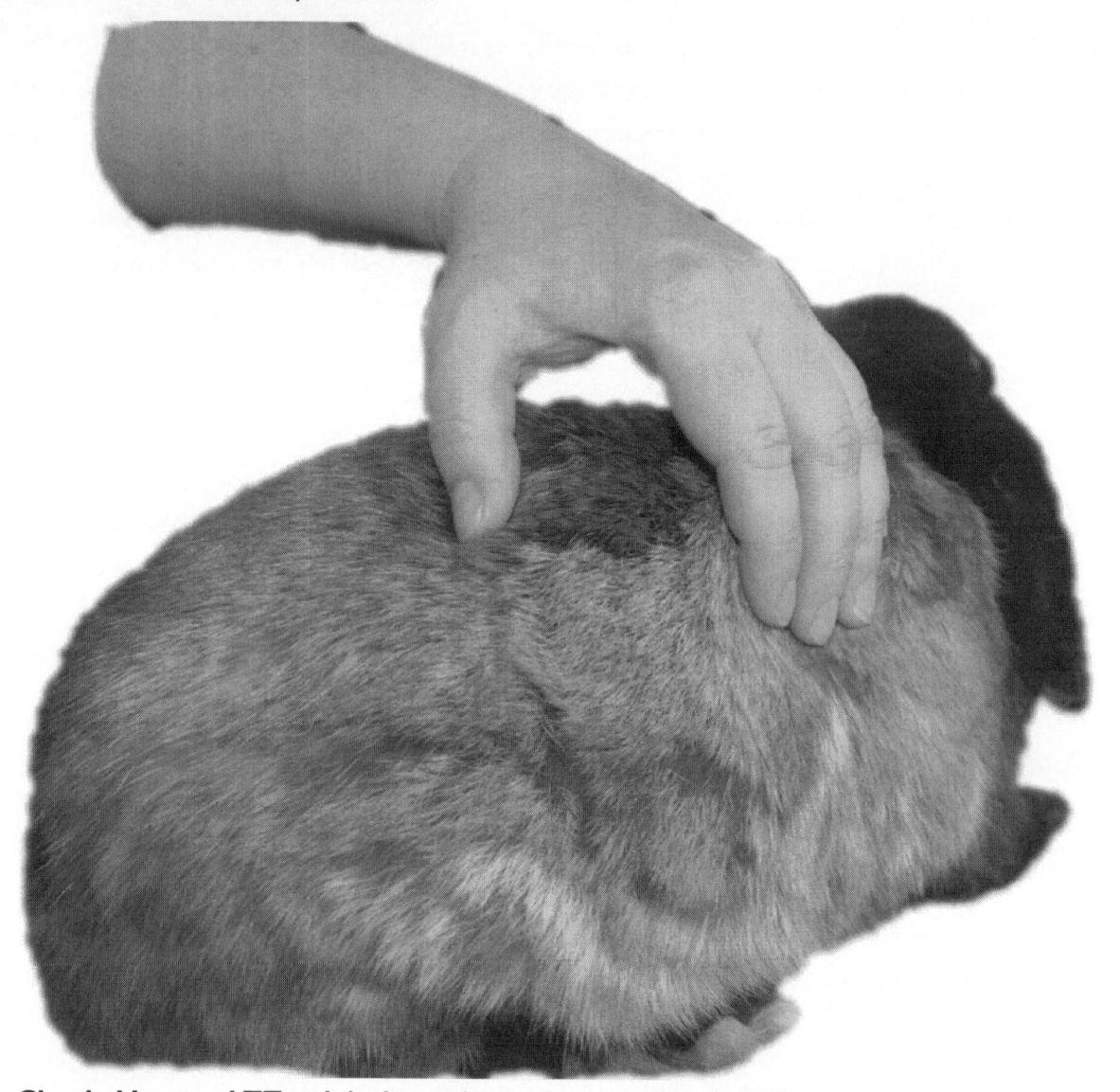

The Clouded Leopard TTouch is the easiest to learn and is the TTouch from which all the others evolved. Notice how only the pads of the fingers are used to make the one and a quarter circle of the skin.

With your pet on you lap, or in an easy to reach position, use your least dominant hand to contain your pet gently. Next, imagine a clock face on the opposite side of your pet's body to the side being contained. The size of the clock you imagine will vary depending on the animal you are TTouching, but around a centimetre in diameter is a good start. When you imagine the numbers of the clock, it important to ensure that 6 on the clock is located at the lowest point of gravity. For example, if you were to imagine the clock face on the side of a guinea pig that was in a normal standing position with all four feet on the ground, 6 on the clock would be found near the ground, and 12 on the clock would be near its top line.

The Clouded Leopard TTouch is suitable for many different pets and is one of the most commonly used TTouches.

Using your dominant hand, place the pads of your fingers gently on your pet's body, at 6 on the clock on your imaginary clock face; your thumb can be placed on your pet's body in a natural position to act as a support. Push the skin (in a clockwise direction) lightly up to 12 on the clock, back round the clock face to 6 on the clock, continue this movement and stop at around 8 or 9 on the clock. Ensure all 4 fingers make the circle as many people forget to move their little finger. Without taking your fingers off your pet's body, take time to pause, allowing your pet's central nervous system to process the information this circle has provided. Slide your fingers to another location on your pet's body and repeat. Deciding where to perform the next circle will really depend on the reaction your pet gives you. You can either slide to a random area to perform the next circle or perform the circles in connected lines along your pet's body, from nose to tail. As well as TTouching your pet's body, you can also TTouch your pet's head, ears, face, paws, abdomen and tail. Each TTouch provides your pet's central nervous system with new information and therefore it is important to try to TTouch your pet in as many different locations as you can.

When moving the skin, it is important to ensure you use just enough pressure for the skin to move but not so little as to slide over the skin. Equally, the key to the effectiveness of the TTouch movements is the lightness of the circles. If you use too much pressure, the central nervous system does not process the information in the same way it also isn't overly comfortable for your pet and it may try to get away. Be careful not to see TTouch as a form of massage. Whilst giving the TTouch, it is important to keep your wrist as loose and straight as possible. If you are finding it tricky making light circles, take note of the position of your wrist. If your wrist is bent, much of your fine motor control is lost, resulting in a less fluid circle being made. Try to keep your wrist as straight yet relaxed as you can. If your pet appears to be twitchy or worried, adjust the pressure and/or speed of your circles. Remember, slow and light circles are the most effective.

PRESSURE EXERCISE – HOW MUCH PRESSURE SHOULD YOU USE?

Our small pets are delicate creatures and so our TTouches should be also – to see how much pressure is needed when giving the TTouches, try the following exercise.

Use your finger to move the skin of your cheek, at the top, just below your eye, with such gentle pressure that you can barely feel your cheek bone underneath. It is important to ensure that enough pressure is used to move the skin but not so much that your cheek bone is very noticeable. If you can feel the bone then you are using too much pressure for our sensitive small pets.

How fast should I make my circles?

Getting the speed of your TTouches right takes time and practice, as a rule of thumb, each circle should take around two seconds from start to finish. On occasion, you may need to make your circles a little faster to begin with, especially if the animal you are TTouching is very active. If this is the case, start with circles that take around one second to complete, ensuring you make a distinct pause at the end of each circle and slowly increase the length of time each circle takes. You will find that as your circles slow down, so does your pet.

Noah's March

Noah's March is a series of long connected strokes used often used to start and end a session and helps to integrate your pet's body. It helps our small pets to feel connected from nose and tail and helps to bring together the TTouches they have already received. Being so tiny, our small pets may find the close connection on Noah's March a little worrying to use at the start of a session so I would recommend that it only be used to end a session. With nervous pets, you may prefer to use the back of your hand and fingers as this is perceived as less threatening.

How to do the Noah's March

In order for Noah's March to be effective, keep your wrist loose and gently stroke the length of your pet, try to feel a connection to your pet through your hand and fingers and visualise a feeling of oneness. There is a real difference between Noah's March and simply stroking your pet, as Noah's March is a mindful and connecting TTouch. If your pet is nervous and will only allow a connection via the TTouch Tools, visualise a connection through the tool and make a similar connected stroke. Some pets will only allow touch in a certain area, it is fine to adjust the length of your Noah's March so as not to scare your pet or use the back of your fingers instead as this feels far less threatening than your palm.

The Racoon TTouch

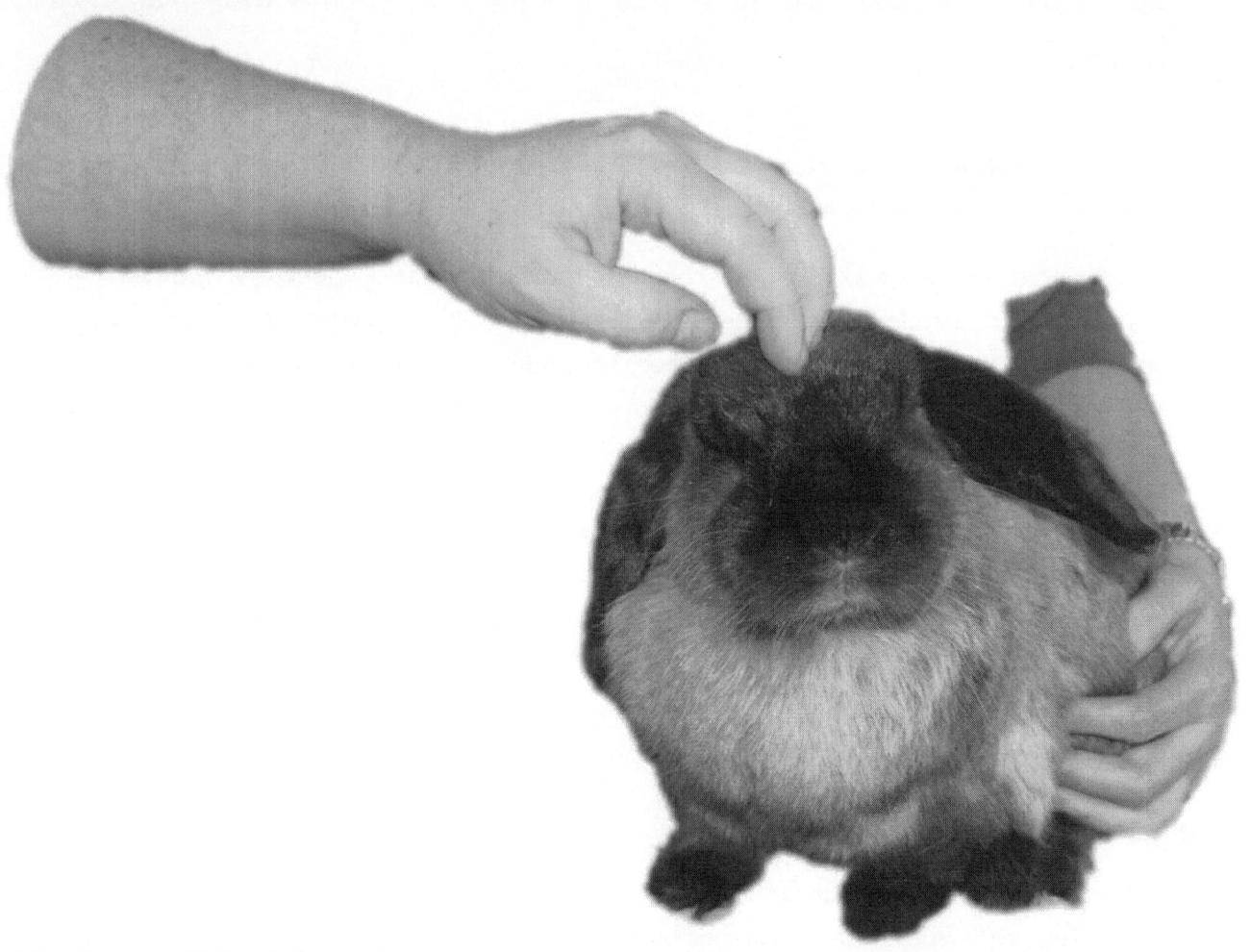

The Raccoon TTouch is particularly suitable for our small pets as it allows you to TTouch very small and delicate areas. Notice how the rabbit is supported with the other hand to keep it balanced and feeling secure.

In order to be able to offer the TTouch to our much tinier companions, we must make sure we adapt our TTouches to fit their much smaller frames. The Racoon TTouch is one such TTouch that is great for our small pets. The Raccoon TTouch was inspired by the dextrous way racoons use their hand-like paws to find their food, especially when dabbling in small streams. It is this dainty, dextrous, lightness that makes this TTouch so perfect for our small pets. The Raccoon TTouch is also great for providing pain relief for old or arthritic pets as well as being great in times of illness or injury. You can use this TTouch on any body part, especially on the head and cheeks.

How to do the Raccoon TTouch

The Racoon TTouch uses the very tips of the fingers to make very tiny one and a quarter circles. Start by bending your fingers at about 90 degrees from your pet's body so only the very tips of your fingers are in contact with your pet. In order that the circles remain light, you must keep the heel and palm of your hand away from your pet's body. The thumb can either remain in contact with your pet or can be taken away if it concerns your pet. The other hand should be used to steady your pet if it is safe to do so.

The Abalone TTouch

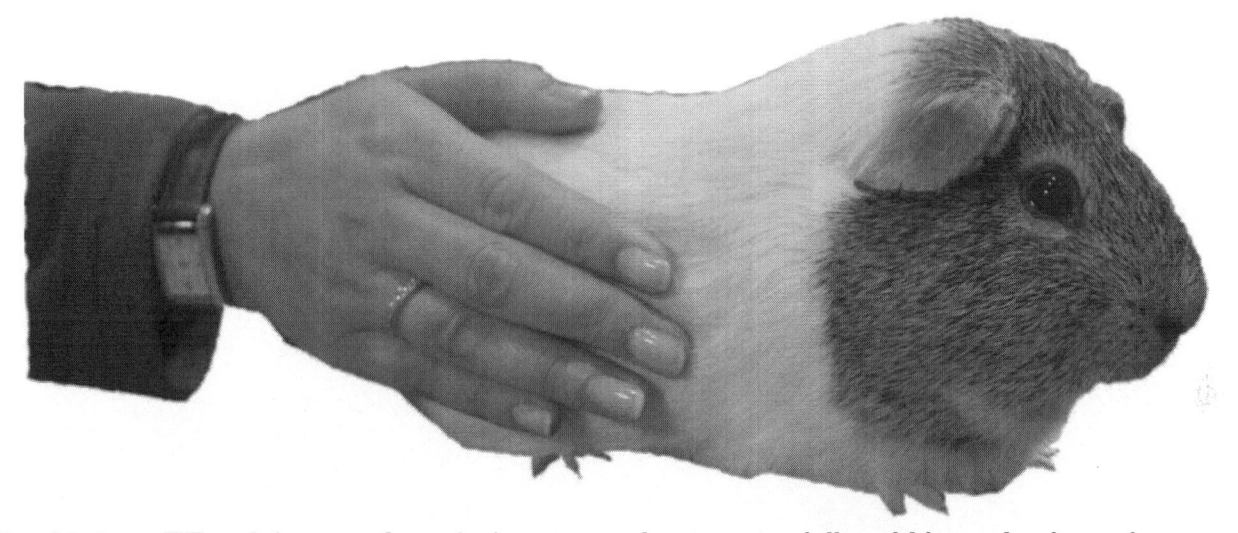

The Abalone TTouch is great for calming stressed pets, especially rabbits and guinea pigs. Notice how the palm curves around the contours of the guinea pig's hind quarters rather than remaining flat and rigid.

The Abalone is a large sea creature, rather like the limpets that can be commonly found in rock pools, stuck fast to the rocks. The Abalone TTouch was named after this strange creature due to the way the hand is placed flat against the animal's body. The Abalone TTouch is great for pets that are nervous of being handled or that suffer from stress easily. This TTouch provides comforting warmth and can be great for older and ill pets and for reducing stress in animals that are visiting the vet. Sadly the Abalone TTouch is reserved for our larger 'small pets' such as large rats, rabbits and guinea pigs.

How to do the Abalone TTouch

Place the flat of your hand on your animal's body, allow it to mould to the contours to ensure it has an even contact. With the palm of your hand, move the skin in the same clockwise one and quarter circle as the previous TTouches. Pause for a moment and then slide your hand to another point and make another circle. Your other hand should be placed on the opposite side of your pet's body to provide support. The warmth of your hand is comforting and calming and this TTouch proves very effective, especially when used on the shoulders. Rabbits especially benefit from the Abalone TTouch as they often develop a lot of tension through the shoulders due to their bottom heavy build. Equally, this TTouch is very useful for teaching rabbits to overcome a fear of being picked up or being groomed.

The Python Lift

Lifting TTouches such as the Python Lift are great for easing tension in the shoulders. Very nervous or flighty rabbits are often very tight in the shoulders and hind quarters.

The Python Lift came about whilst Linda Tellington-Jones was working with a sickly python called Joyce. Snakes move in a very interesting way with undulating movements of the skin and muscle. Linda tried to mimic this movement using her hands on the snake's body. This TTouch proved very beneficial and has shown to be wonderful for relieving tension in many species, including people!

The Python Lift is great for young animals as it helps with coordination and body awareness, older animals can benefit too as it helps to improve ailing circulation. Fearful animals can experience renewed self confidence and can become less scared of loud or unexpected noises (such as fireworks)

How to do the Python Lift

Place your lightly curved fingers on your animal's body whilst your other hand is placed on the opposite side of your pet's body to act as a support. Using a very light pressure, use your curved fingers to gently and slowly support the skin upwards for a few millimetres. Next, without taking your hand off your pet, pause with the skin and muscle supported for a few seconds, remembering to breathe in order to stay relaxed. Once you have paused, slowly carry the skin back downwards to where you began; allow this release to take another five seconds. Don't be alarmed if the skin naturally moves beyond the area that you started on, this is perfectly normal, however it is important that you don't drag the skin downwards as this will be uncomfortable for your pet and can actually increase your pet's tension. During the Python Lift, allow your thumb to rest in a natural position on your pet's body.

The number of fingers you use to make the Python Lift will depend on the size of the animal and the area you are TTouching. With a rabbit, guinea pig or large rat, it is possible to use all of your fingers, however anything smaller, will require you to use only a couple, or even just your index finger.

The Llama TTouch

Many animals find the sight of an open hand rather unnerving. Making contact with the back of your hand is much less threatening.

The Llama TTouch may come as a surprise as it is performed with the back of the hand. Pets that are afraid of being touched often find being touched with back of the hand far less threatening than being touched with the palm of the hand or fingers. It may be that they instinctively realise that the back of the hand is unable to grab them.

How to do the Llama TTouch

Using a very light pressure, make the same one and quarter circles using the back of the fingers, this is especially useful around the head and shoulders.

The Chimp TTouch (and the Baby Chimp TTouch)

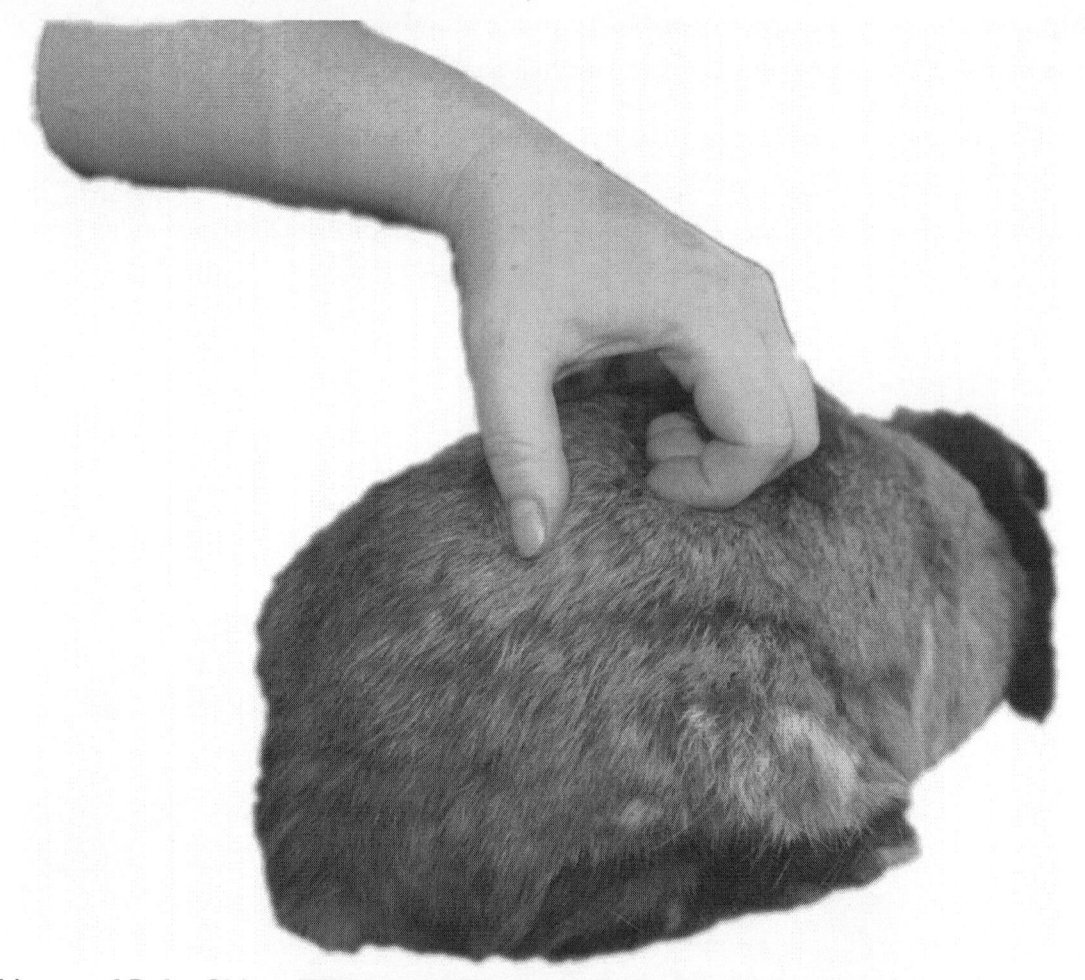

The Chimp and Baby Chimp TTouches are great for pets that are afraid of being touched. If you suffer from arthritis or stiff joints, you may find these two TTouches easier than using the front of your hands. Many people who find the other TTouches tricky to coordinate not only find these TTouches easier but find that their own hand mobility increases, resulting in the other TTouches becoming easier too.

These two TTouches are in a way similar to the larger Llama TTouch as they employ the back of your hand rather than the palm. In this way, very sensitive or fearful pets are less afraid of your approach as they understand you are unable to grab them with your hand in this way. Pets that have been abused or have had little contact with people often benefit from these TTouches and can quickly learn to trust people once more. This is also a great TTouch to learn if you are finding the other TTouches tricky to coordinate or if you suffer from arthritis or stiff joints.

How to do the Chimp (and Baby Chimp) TTouch.

Curl your fingers towards your palm and use the back of your fingers to make small and light one and a quarter circles on your pet. The Chimp TTouch uses the area between the first and second finger joint and is helpful for larger pets or for TTouching larger areas. The Baby Chimp TTouch uses the area between the finger tip and first finger joint and is therefore more useful for our small pets or for TTouching smaller or more specific areas.

The Ear TTouch – **The TTouch that saves lives!**

The Ear TTouch could save your pet's life. It has been shown to stabilise blood pressure and heart rate in time of shock or illness.

There are few parts of an animal as tactile as the ears and it is well known that both animals and people get great enjoyment from stroking them. However, did you know that stroking your pet's ears can actually be life saving? Stroking the ears, from the base to the tip has been shown to stabilise the heart rate and blood pressure in pets suffering from shock.

Shock is a lack of adequate blood flow to meet the body's needs. Adequate blood flow requires effective heart pumping, open intact vessels and sufficient blood volume to maintain flow and pressure. Any condition adversely affecting the heart, vessels or blood volume can induce shock. With our small pets, even a minor accident can induce shock as well as many medical conditions such a gastric problems e.g. Gastrointestinal Stasis in rabbits

At first the body attempts to compensate for the inadequate circulation by speeding up the heart, constricting the skin vessels and maintaining fluid in the circulation by reducing output of urine. This becomes increasingly difficult to do when the vital organs aren't getting enough oxygen to carry on these activities. After a time, shock becomes self-perpetuating. Prolonged shock causes death.

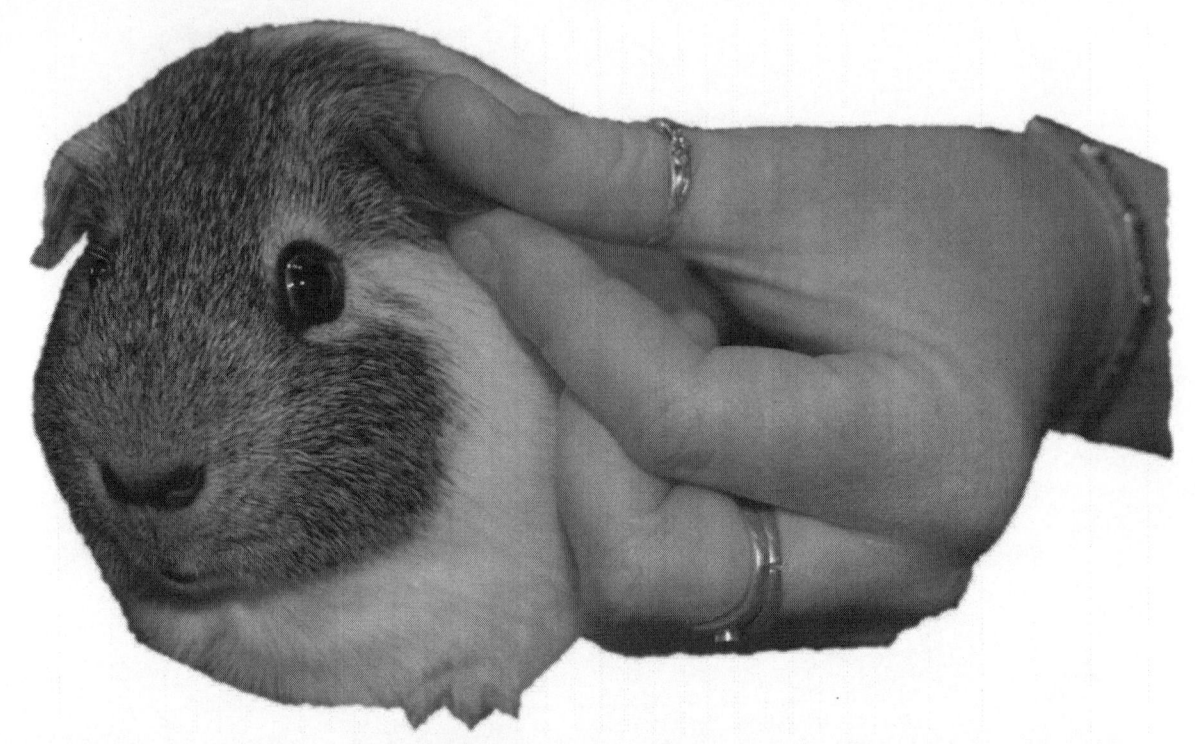

Ears of all shapes and sizes can be TTouched. In Traditional Chinese Medicine, it is said that there are specific points on the ear that relate to every other body part, especially the digestion. This makes the Ear TTouch invaluable in cases of colic or other digestive upset.

The Ear TTouch is also used to calm and reduce fear and stress and is often used as a session starting point for many of our small pets. Small pets that have difficulty in calming down when handled can find this TTouch very relaxing. Rabbits, guinea pigs and rats in particular enjoy the Ear TTouch, mainly due to their sociable nature; these areas are used in social interaction between members of the same social group and to strengthen friendship bonds.

The Ear TTouch is very useful to give before and after surgery as it can help to aid with pain relief, to speed healing and to stabilise the circulation

How to do the Ear TTouch

Ears come in all shapes and sizes and therefore the way in which you TTouch the ears will depend on the animal you are TTouching.

How to TTouch the ears of rabbits and adult guinea pigs

Unless you are TTouching your animal's ears in an emergency, it is important to introduce your animal to TTouch before TTouching the ears.

Simply start with some Raccoon TTouches on the head and at the base of the ears, ensuring your pet is happy with this area being touched.

Gently hold the ear, with the knuckle of your bent index finger on the underside of the ear and your thumb on top. Treat the ear as if it were a rose petal taking the utmost care. Gently and slowly slide from the base of the ear to the tip, ensuring you slide the entire length of the ear and smoothly slide off the tip. Repeat this sliding movement four times.

With lop eared rabbits, the ear should be supported horizontally for the duration of the slide and must not be allowed to drop down suddenly. As for up-eared rabbits and guinea pigs, simply slide in the direction the ear points.

You may also incorporate the circular movements by gently circling the ears at their base, this has been shown to reduce tension across the forehead and scalp; which in turn reduces reactivity to movement in animals with a tendency to be snappy or to panic at fast moving objects.

How to TTouch the ears of hamsters, mice, gerbils and rats

Even pets with tiny ears can enjoy the Ear TTouch. Be sure to make your TTouches feather light as the ears are very delicate.

Our smaller pets understandably have smaller ears and therefore the ear slides and TTouches must be far smaller, this doesn't mean they are any less effective. If using your fingers, use just the very tip of your thumb and index finger to circle the ear at its base and to gently slide from the base to the tip.

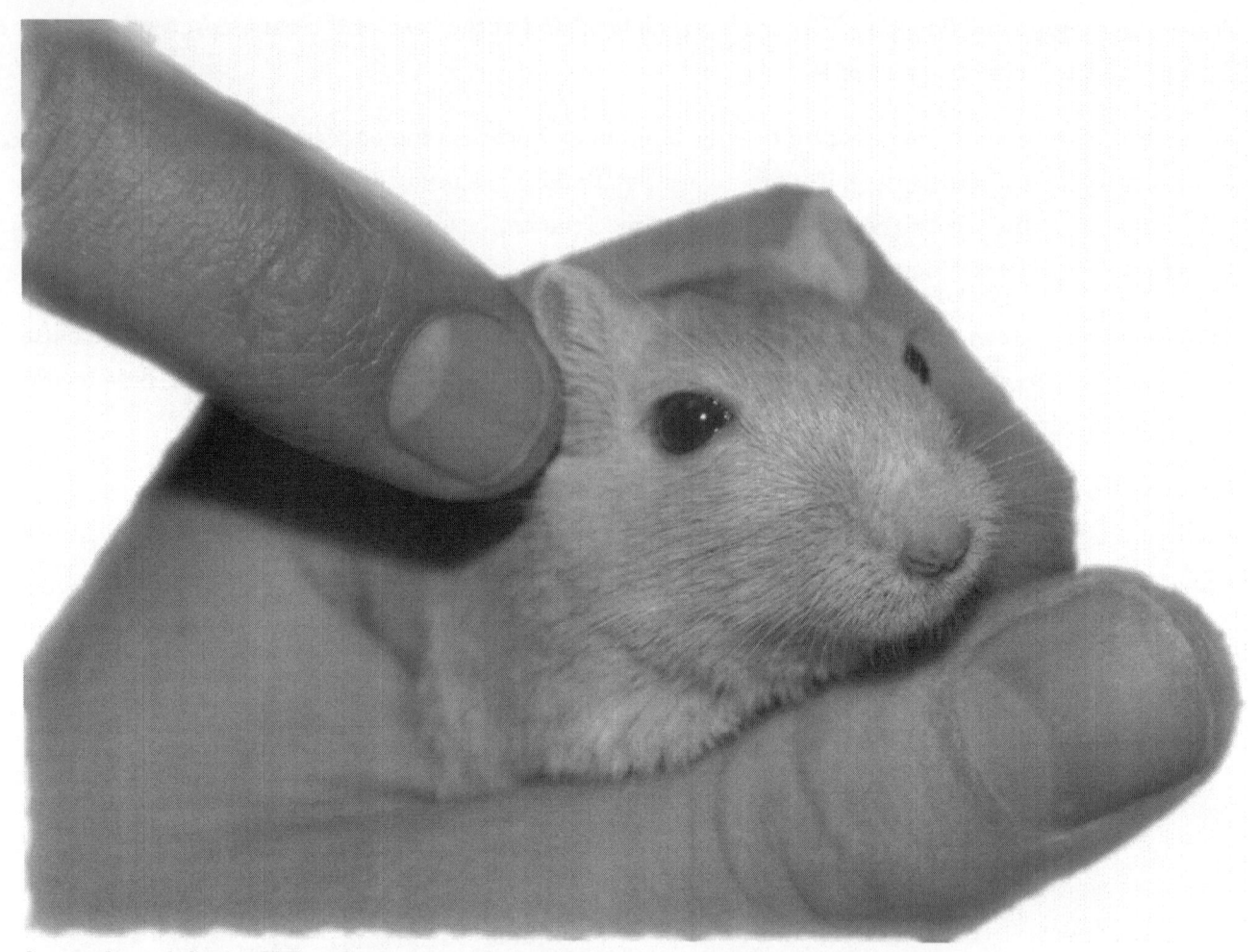

It can be tricky to TTouch the ears of gerbils, mice, rats and hamsters. You may prefer to use a paintbrush or cotton bud (Q-tip) instead.

With many of our smaller pets, this may be a little intimidating so it may be useful to use a soft artist's paint brush or cotton bud (Q-tip) to stroke the ear, again from the base to the tip or to make small one and a quarter circles. Repeat this sliding movement about four times.

The Tail TTouch

The differences between the tails of our small pets is staggering, from the long and prehensile tails of rats and mice to the small and fluffy tails of rabbits, not forgetting our tailless guinea pigs! These differences directly relate to the life style of our pets as each is used in a different way.

Rats and mice, with their highly mobile tails, love to climb and employ their tails rather like a fifth limb to help with balance and stability.

Rabbits on the other hand, in the wild, live in open grassy habitats, where their naturally gleaming white tails are used to 'flash' a warning of danger to others in the group.

Wild guinea pigs live in long grass, where a tail would be hindrance and therefore they have lost their tail entirely.

Hamsters too have almost lost their tails for similar reasons, the remaining tail is known as a vestigial organ.

The tail, especially in mice and rats, can often help to indicate areas of tension through the back as, in many animals it is known to mirror the kinks, bends and twists of the spine. With our canine friends for example, a bend at the base of the tail may indicate tension in the neck area whilst a bend at the tip may indicate tension through the pelvis. It is likely that this will ring true when it comes to rats and mice. Many older male rats will have a myriad of bends and kinks in their tail that arise as they become older and less mobile. Many of our pets use their tails to aid in balance, and any tension in the tail can cause aggression and nervousness as they feel an overall sensation of imbalance.

The Tail TTouch is useful to aid in nervousness and aggression as well as sensitivity to being lifted or to loud noises.

How to do the Tail TTouch?

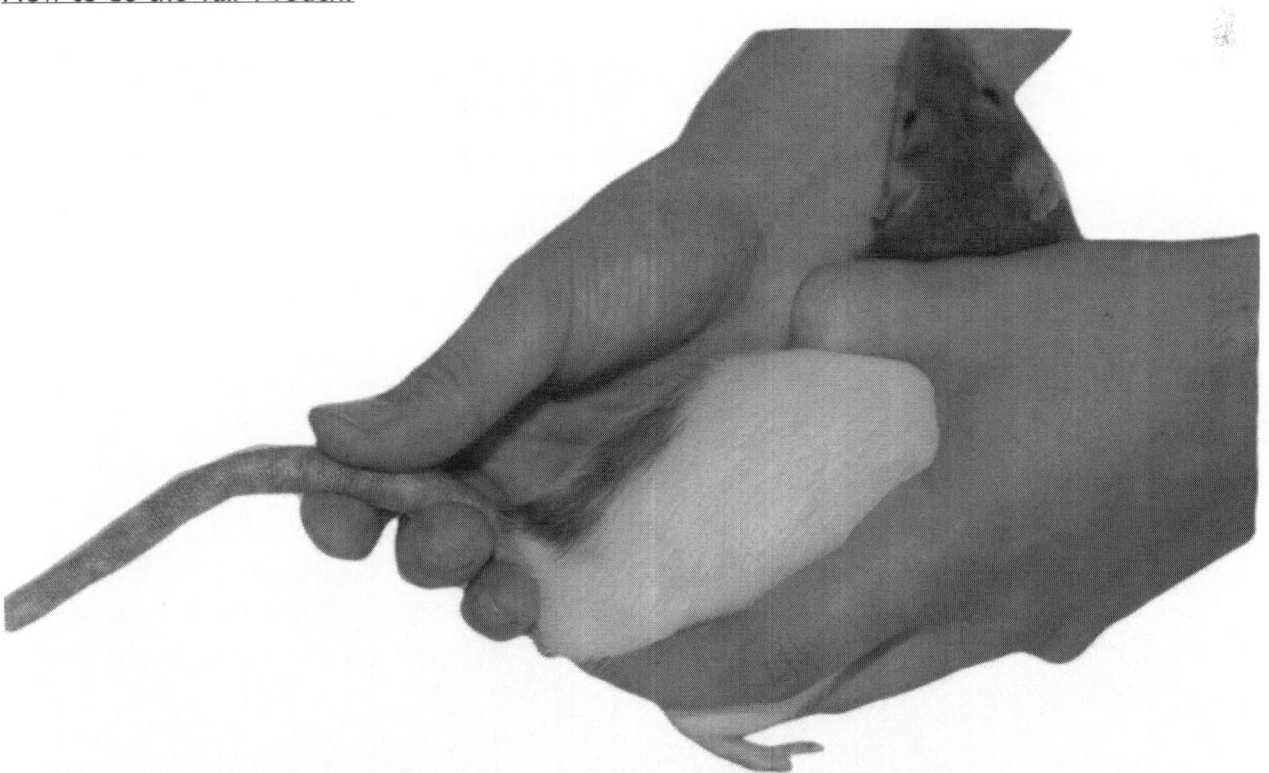

The Tail TTouch has been shown to help with nervousness and aggression. It can also help animals suffering from aching joints associated with old age or illness.

The tail can be TTouched in a variety of ways. To start with ensure your pet has all four feet on a solid surface (or your lap) so that it has the ability to move if it feels like it. If your pet is on your lap, it is better to allow it to stand on a cushion as this gives a more stable and level surface and allows your pet to feel more grounded.

Slowly and gently stroke the tail from the base to the tip, feeling for any bumps or kinks. After a few strokes, gently undulate the tail as you again stroke from the base to the tip. The undulating movement must be only a small amount and you must be extremely gentle. Never force the tail in a direction it does not want to go as not only is this painful for your pet but it is likely to increase your pet's tension. Many pets enjoy having the tail moved in very small circles at the base; you can also incorporate some Clouded Leopard and Raccoon TTouches at the base and along the length of the tail too.

As guinea pigs obviously lack tails, it can be useful to TTouch around the pelvis and hind end. If your small pet has lost its tail or has a part missing, the Tail TTouch can provide a release from old tension caused at the time of the injury. It is believed that some pets can experience a form of phantom limb pain if they have lost all or part of the tail.

Using tools to help your pet. Great for pets that cannot be touched by hand

This rabbit is afraid of being touched. Here we see Adam using two TTouch Wands to initiate contact without invading its personal space and reinforcing its fear.

So far you have discovered how you can use the TTouch technique to benefit your pet's behaviour and well being but what if your pet is too scared to be picked up or is aggressive?

Many nervous or aggressive pets are not necessarily afraid of people but more of being **handled** by people. Being picked up can be very scary for our small pets, especially when you consider just how frightening a hand must appear when it comes looming over them. Also, many pets may have been mishandled either by the breeder or in the case of rescued animals, by a previous owner. Experience shows that the majority of small pets with a fear of people have in fact developed a fear of hands rather than contact with people in general.

TTouch is especially beneficial for these frightened pets as it allows them to experience a whole new way of interacting with people and helps them quickly overcome their preconceptions. However, a whole new approach is needed to ensure that they are not stressed and therefore able to learn that handling is not as scary as they once thought. This is where a selection of household objects are used to make 'tools' to initiate touch.

You may be surprised to learn that many nervous pets are actually not afraid of people but rather have learned to be afraid of being touched. Using TTouch Tools to initiate contact can be a real eye opener. Many pets that run at the sight of an approaching hand are more than happy to be touched with a tool.

The TTouch technique is used not only in rescue centres but also in zoos and wildlife parks across the world with animals that are either too scared or too dangerous to be touched by hand. In order that these animals can benefit from this technique, a number of tools are used to keep the animal calm and the person safe. In fact, even with pets that are happy to be handled, using tools can be a very polite way of introducing the TTouch technique, a little like shaking hands with a stranger.

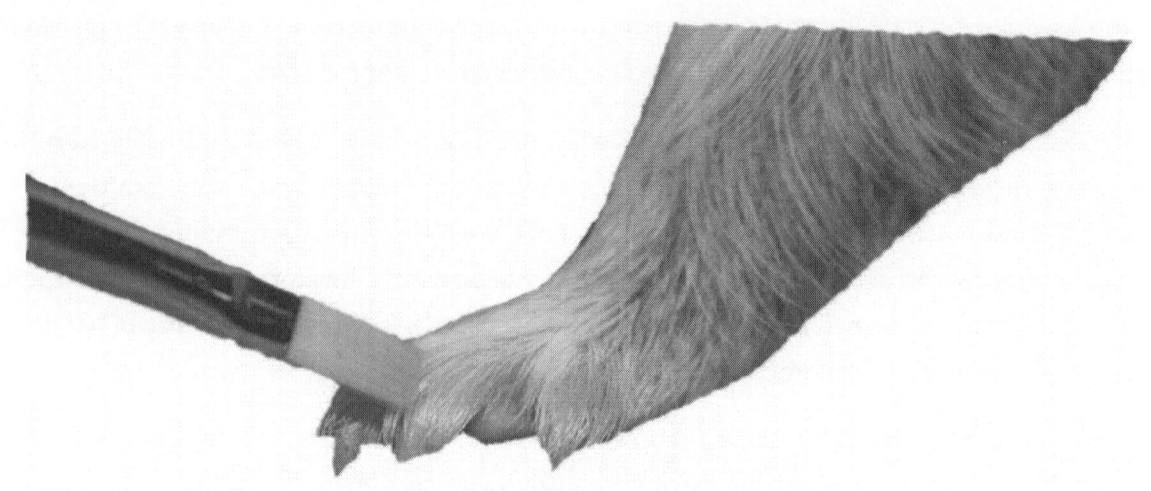

Using TTouch tools allows you to offer TTouches to areas that are far too small for a finger to be effective. Here we see a paintbrush being used on a guinea pig's toes.

There are many different tools to choose from, many of which you may already have. There is no need to spend lots of money on expensive products; the local discount shop will reap big rewards! The only rules to consider; the tool must be safe if chewed and must be replaceable if broken.

I recommend having a selection of artists paint brushes, pipe cleaners, rubber tipped pencils (using the rubber end) cotton buds (Q-tips) millet sprays, non-toxic fruit tree twigs and feathers.

How to use the tools

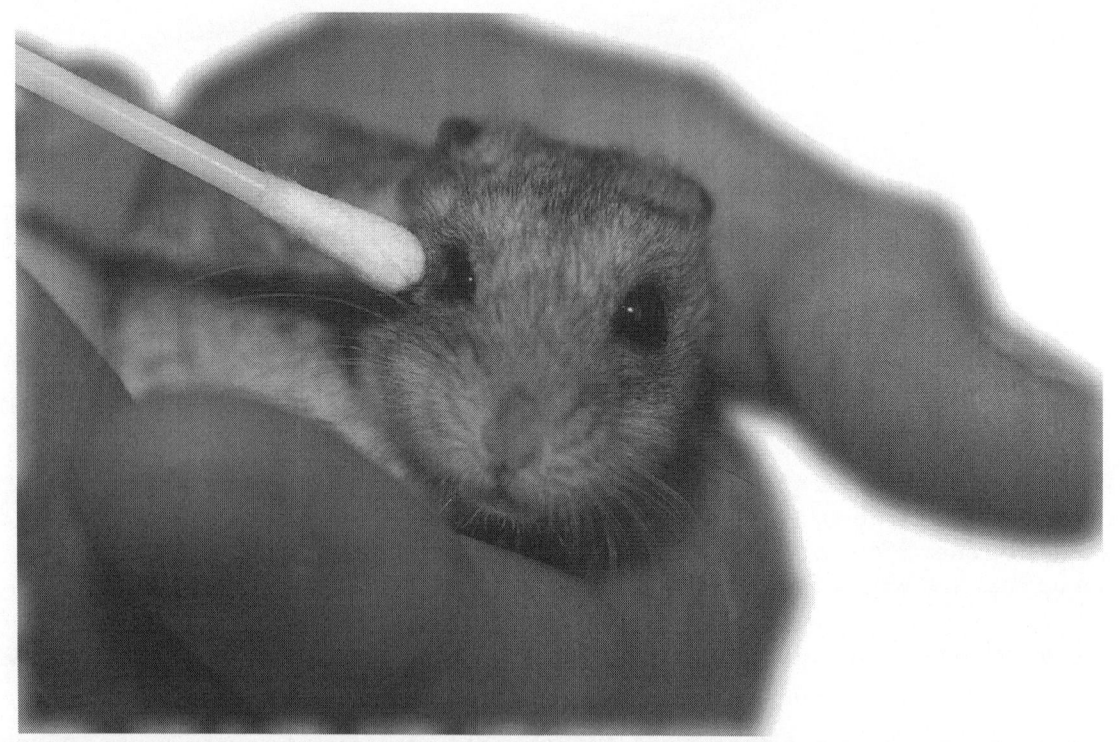

This tiny Chinese hamster is being TTouched with a cotton bud (Q-tip) Initially he would bite when held but soon learned that being with people could be enjoyable.

How you start a session with tools will depend on the level of fear your pet has. However, as a rule, if your pet is so scared that it continually runs away out of reach, it is far better to contain it in a cage or carrier. Continually having to chase your pet from one end of its enclosure to the other will only increase your pet's stress level; it is also unlikely to learn any new responses as it will be reacting in an instinctive manner.

When you have your pet contained, calmly approach your pet with a paintbrush or feather and watch your pet's reaction. If your pet becomes scared, you may need to make your tools a little longer with a length of dowel or garden cane, so the distance between you can be increased. If this is the case, first try a different tool; it may be the type of tool you were using that caused your pet to be worried.

Initially, before touching your pet with your chosen tool, calmly stroke the bars of its cage or carrier with the tool, two or three times and then back off. This may seem a very bizarre thing to do, but in fact, stroking the bars of its cage is actually reassuring for your pet. The key reason being the fact that a non-threatening approach was made and then removed without contact being made and without your pet being stressed. By ensuring your pet remains stress free, most pets quickly realise that the tools are not to be feared.

Once your pet is happy for you to stroke the cage bars, you can then more to initially stroke the air above your pet with your chosen tool. Although you are not touching your pet it is important that you are just as slow and mindful as you would be when making physical contact. Next, begin stroking your pet mindfully and gently along its entire body. Resist the temptation to carry on, but rather back off straight away in a slow and calm manner. Just like stroking the bars of the cage, this non-threatening approach teaches your pet that contact is actually not that scary. Depending on the extent of your pet's fear, you may wish to repeat this initial procedure several times. Next begin to stroke your pet calmly, concentrating in areas that it finds comfortable. Stroke the whiskers against its face and around the base of the ears. This is very soothing.

If your pet appears comfortable, start to use the tools to make small one and a quarter circles, in the same way as the circular TTouches mentioned earlier, making sure you watch your pet's reaction at all times. You may need to use two tools, especially with rats and rabbits as their inquisitive nature means they often nibble and chew at the tools being used. By using two tools at one, your pet can be distracted with one tool whilst enjoying TTouches with the other. Remember, small pets have a very short attention span so it is important to give them many small breaks to process the experiences. Experience shows that pets that are allowed time to process the information they receive during these sessions actually improve much faster than those that are not. If your pet appears to be twitchy or worried, adjust the pressure and/or speed of your circles. Remember, slow and light circles are the most effective.

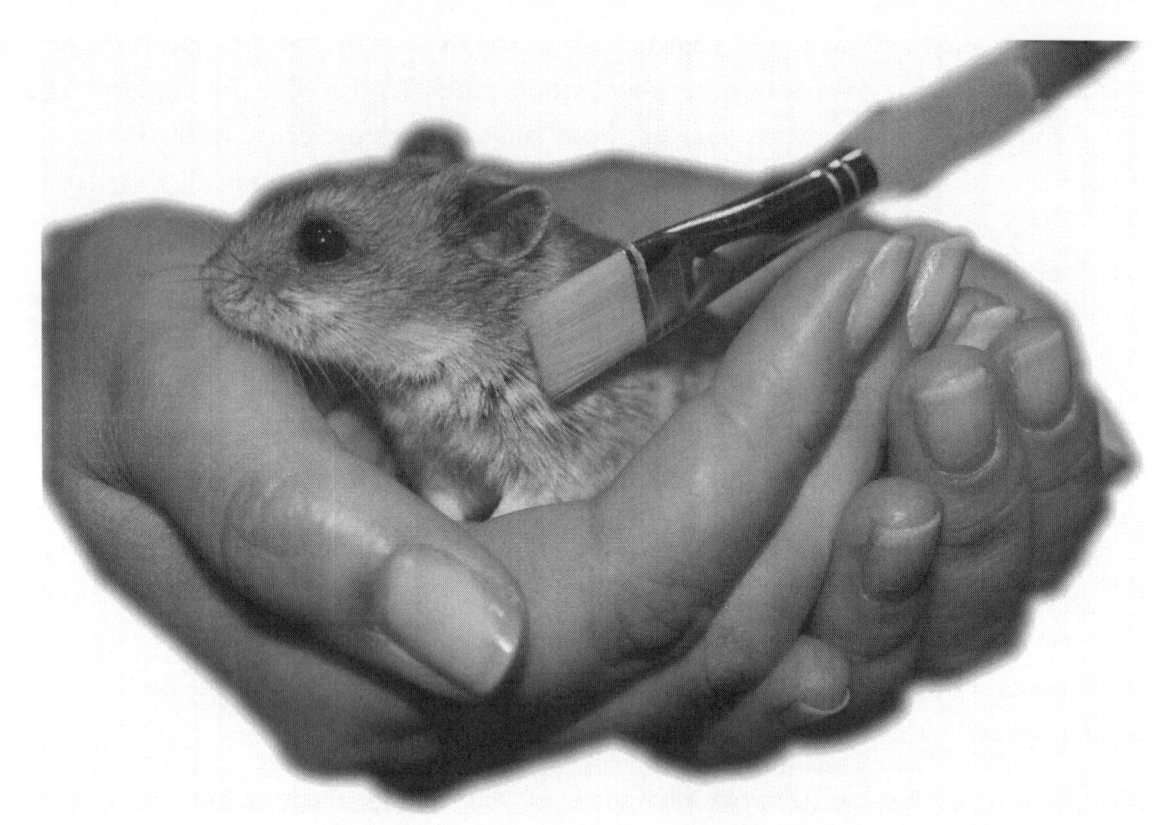

Notice how this hamster is gently contained in cupped hands rather than being restrained. It is important that you offer your pet the freedom to move as being restrained can be very scary. It also enables you to observe how your pet reacts to having different areas touched.

Over time, you can slowly reduce the length of the tool, decreasing the distance between your hand and your pet's body. It is important not to rush, however, many pets react in such a positive manner that you can start to use your hand to touch them very quickly.

Every pet is different, and the time it takes to be able to introduce your hand will vary. When you do so, start by stroking with the back of your hand (the Llama TTouch or Chimp TTouch). Experience is likely to have taught your pet that open hands can grab and therefore are to be avoided at all costs. By approaching in this totally new fashion, with the back of your hand, animals appear to instinctively recognise that they are safe.

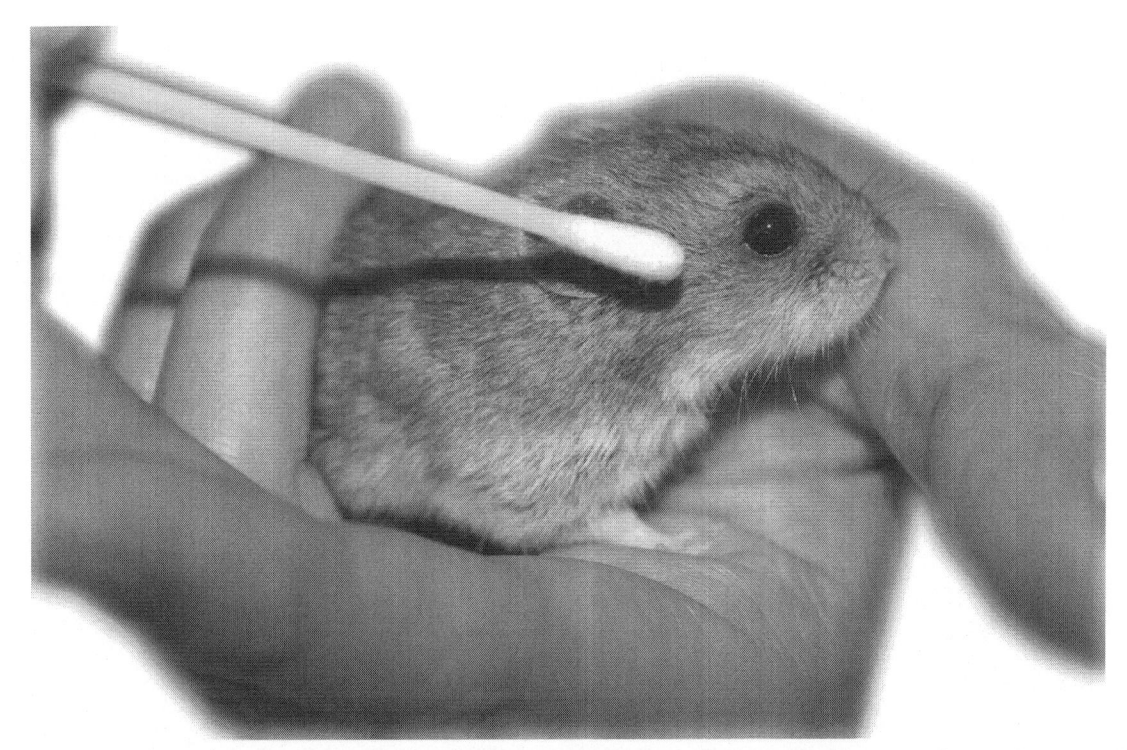

Many pets learn to accept the Tools in a very short space of time. Before you know it you will be able to use a finger instead. However, let your pet dictate the pace and never be tempted to rush.

Where on my pet's body can I use the TTouch techniques?

Everywhere! Each TTouch will have a profound effect on your pet and tension will be reduced. If you notice your pet is unhappy at you touching a specific area or body part, you can slowly introduce the TTouches to this area. To begin with, it may only be possible to offer one TTouch on a particularly sensitive area per session. This is fine. In fact, it is possible to create positive change much more quickly if you do not over TTouch such areas. It would appear that the central nervous system can become overwhelmed if you try to do so.

Each animal is an individual, therefore, what works for one may not work for another. With this in mind, it is useful to really get to know your pet, offer TTouches to areas that you may initially think have no connection to the behaviour it is showing. You may be surprised by the results.

How often should I use TTouch?

The TTouch can be used as often as you like provided you do not make the sessions too long. Small animals have very short attention spans and therefore short but regular sessions are certainly better then two or three very long ones. It is also important to use a variety of TTouches to ensure the sessions remain non-habitual.

How quickly should I see a change in my pet's behaviour?

Some pets will show dramatic changes in a matter of minutes whereas others may take a little longer.

How to start and end a session

It is important to ensure you are as calm and relaxed as possible before you start a TTouch session with your pet. Animals of all shapes and sizes are able to sense our breathing and heart rate variability and if we are tense and stressed, so will they be. Start with taking some very slow and deep breaths, taking your time to exhale and clear your mind. Make sure you sit on a chair or cushion to insure the area where you intend to TTouch your pet is comfortable, if you are forced to sit on a cold floor you are unlikely to feel relaxed.

Start (if appropriate) and end with the Noah's March TTouch, this soothing TTouch helps to calm your pet and to integrate its front and back end and prepares your pet's body for the session to come. It also helps to consolidate any experiences its nervous system has had during the session.

Chapter 9 – Common behaviour problems

Tips for troubled pets

Small pets can suffer from many different behavioural problems and a whole new book would be needed to include them all. It is important to understand that every animal is an individual and therefore each may have its own unique reason for the behaviour it is displaying. It has become far too commonplace for animal behaviourists to take a one size fits all approach when dealing with common behavioural issues. As an example, many behaviourists attempt to cure rabbits that show fear aggression, by wearing protective clothing and rewarding the rabbit when it stops attacking. This technique does nothing to increase the rabbit's confidence and trust in people, it only teaches the rabbit that attacking does not stop interaction. Equally it does nothing to address any discomfort the rabbit may be in due to the experiences it has had in the past. Solving behaviour issues in any animal is complex. It takes time and patience and a holistic approach, to ensure the root cause of the behaviour is addressed, rather than just treating the symptoms.

With this in mind, this chapter contains general guides to some specific, common behaviour issues. If your pet is not responding to the tips shown, it is important to ensure you have evaluated the situation carefully. If you are at all unsure, it is wise to consult a professional for advice.

Common rabbit behaviour problems

Resistance to being picked up

Many rabbits, although friendly in general, will show resistance to being picked up. When the rabbit is lifted it may retaliate by biting, scratching, kicking violently or generally just getting in a mad panic.

Why does it occur?

A fear of being picked up usually stems from a lack of socialisation as a youngster and/or a scary and often painful experience earlier in life. Rabbits are ground loving creatures and being lifted off the ground is a very scary experience and totally alien to their way of life. Therefore they must **learn** to accept being picked up as their instincts tell them to avoid being lifted at all costs. If a rabbit has been mishandled as a youngster they can develop painful areas on the spine, or although not physically injured, they may retain a fear of the pain they experienced initially. Pain or fear of pain, are two of the greatest barriers to learning, and these must be overcome if your pet is to learn to accept being picked up. Baby rabbits are small and easy to handle and as such, often get handled very roughly. Young animals are like sponges, soaking up and learning new experiences day by day. Any rough handling can bring on a fear of being picked up that can continue in to adulthood.

Which TTouches may help?

Clouded Leopard, Abalone, Python Lift

What can I do to help?

Helping your rabbit to overcome this fear can take a long time and it is important not to rush things. Many people misguidedly believe that simply **forcing** a rabbit to be handled will teach it to accept being picked up. In reality all this does is cause it undue stress and fear and in fact can be a barrier to learning. When stressed, animals release a hormone known as Adrenocorticotropic hormone or ACTH which also causes increased cortisone levels. These hormones have the unusual effect of hindering learning on a conscious level. When these hormones are released the rabbit's brain acts instinctively. These instinctive reactions may be to panic and try to get away or in some cases to freeze stock still. When this happens, many people mistakenly believe their pet is happy and content, when in reality it is scared and has become shut down.

As loving pet owners, we all want the best for our pets and a relationship based on mutual trust and understanding is far preferable to one based on fear and domination. By following the steps outlined below it is possible to teach your rabbit to learn to trust you and to realise that being picked up is not as scary as they once thought.

Session 1

Please note: The following exercise should ideally use a two inch Ace bandage. This is a type of elasticated support bandage that has just the right amount if stretch to make this exercise super effective. However, as not everyone is likely to have these at home, we have described how to use a tea towel instead. Ace bandages are not expensive and can be purchased online.

This may take several sessions. In order to help a fearful rabbit to learn that being picked up is not a fearful experience it is important to use a combination of the TTouches shown above to help your rabbit to become relaxed before you start. Start with a connecting and calming Noah's March and then use gentle Clouded Leopard TTouches around the head and shoulders and slow gentle Python Lifts and Abalone along the barrel. If your pet is afraid of these TTouches then you may prefer to use Llama TTouch and Chimp TTouch instead.

Notice how this rabbit is tense through the neck. His head is tilted at a slight angle. This is causing him to be afraid of being picked up as he finds it uncomfortable.

With your rabbit safely in an open topped box or carrier and once your rabbit is calm, take a tea towel and fold it lengthways until it is about 2 inches wide, slide the tea towel gently under your rabbit's body so you are left with an end at each side. Gently take hold of each end of the tea towel and very slowly and gently take up the slack, causing the tea towel to become a little taut. Hold this tension for three seconds and slowly release the tension. Slide the tea towel down by around one centimetre, once again take up the slack and repeat.

Release the towel at both ends and offer the same TTouches and mentioned earlier, finishing with a calming Noah's March. WITHOUT picking your rabbit up, transfer it back to its enclosure and offer it something tasty to eat.

Session 2 – The following day

At the next session, repeat the steps as shown in the first session, once this is done, and provided your rabbit is calm, gently take up the slack once more but take up more slack on one side and gently lift by three or four centimetres causing a gentle rolling movement. As before, slowly release the tension. Repeat this movement three times and then repeat on the other side, provided your rabbit remains calm. If you have a very young or particularly small rabbit, the lift you create will need to be only one and a half centimetres.

The gentle rolling movement of the wrap has helped the wrap to straighten his neck as the tension through the shoulders has lessened. Notice how his head is now much straighter and his ears are more level.

By using the tea towel to create these gentle lifts, you are not only releasing tension held throughout your pet's underside and back but you are allowing your pet to experience the feeling of being lifted in a safe and secure way. This has the effect of changing the way your rabbit perceives being picked up and allows a trusting relationship to develop. Many behaviour problems can be resolved by chunking the situation down into manageable bite size pieces. The safe and secure lifting movements serve this purpose well whilst addressing the underlying tension.

You may need to repeat these sessions over a period of several weeks or in some cases just a few days, each rabbit is different. Once you are happy your rabbit is ready to be lifted, start by having the rabbit sit on a thick towel or blanket. The first time you pick your rabbit up, do so by using the blanket or towel to lift it off the ground briefly but slowly. Judging by its reaction, you may wish to increase the height your rabbit is lifted until you can cradle it in your arms. It is important that you do NOT hold your rabbit on its back as this is **very stressful**. Watch for any signs of distress and don't be afraid to take a step back if you feel you have rushed things. Rabbits are known for their ability to hide their emotions and even a glassy eyed look can be a sign of unease.

Aggression in the form of biting, lunging and growling

Why does it occur?

Aggression, especially on the rabbit's home territory usually stems from a feeling of insecurity rather than dominance as many people believe. An animal that is confident will not worry about you entering its space as it is secure about its surroundings. An insecure individual will not be happy about having its space invaded and therefore, as it has nowhere to run, can only react by being aggressive. There is also a learned element involved as they quickly realise that this tactic works wonders for getting you to go away!

Aggressive rabbits must always have a full veterinary check up, paying extra special attention to the teeth. Your vet must also check the molar teeth to ensure they have not developed sharp spurs. A confident vet will **not** need to sedate your rabbit to check its molars. Rabbits that are in pain very often develop aggressive tendencies and teeth problems are very painful indeed.

Some rabbits may be very confident but show aggression when you enter their enclosure and touch their food bowl. This can be defensive behaviour but most notably demonstrates a lack of trust between you and your pet. Many rabbits like to feel they are in control of their own surroundings and if things are moved around without their permission, they become afraid at losing control. You could say these animals are still afraid, except this is a fear of losing control rather than of people in general.

Which TTouches may help?

These aggressive rabbits need to develop self confidence and also need to learn to accept others entering their space. Start by using the TTouch Tools such as paintbrushes or feathers, attached to a length of wooden dowel if needed, to make a non threatening contact. To start with, you may need to move your rabbit to a carrier, this mimics the feeling of being in its enclosure but as it is in a new context, the rabbit generally will not instinctively wish to attack. The idea of introducing the tools is to initiate contact, not to provoke the rabbit or tease it. It is far better to be successful away from his usual home territory and then to build up to initiating contact in its enclosure.

Also, Llama TTouch, Chimp TTouch, Baby Chimp TTouch, Clouded Leopard TTouch, Racoon TTouch, Abalone TTouch and Python Lift.

What can I do to help?

Before embarking on any TTouch or rehabilitation programme, there are a few factors to consider.

Is your rabbit entire? Un-neutered rabbits have hormones surging through them from a very young age. In the wild they would prove useful in motivating both male and female rabbits to defend their burrows from strangers. This is necessary as those that are the best at defending their burrows are lucky enough to have a burrow at the heart of the warren; those that are weaker and less aggressive are forced to create their own breeding tunnels on the outskirts. These weaker animals have far less breeding success due to predators. In a domestic context there is no need for this behaviour as it causes both the rabbit and its owners, unnecessary stress. For this reason all rabbits should be neutered for their own good. The vast majority of entire rabbits will have behaviour problems of one sort or another, as well as a hugely increased risk of cancer.

Is your rabbit kept alone? Rabbits that are forced to live singly often show aggression, due to the stress that living a single life causes. Rabbits are very social creatures and need an outlet for their sociable nature. Even if kept as house-rabbits, the company of people simply doesn't compare to having another rabbit as a companion. Depression can be the result of this lonely existence and often manifests itself as aggression. Tests have been carried out on herd animals by keeping them isolated for long periods of time; it was shown that levels of the stress hormone Adrenocorticotropic hormone or ACTH rose markedly when they were confined in this way. These hormones can trigger an animal to react instinctively when approached, i.e. to flee, fight or freeze. In a captive environment, the element of flight is often hindered, so the only real option is to attack.

What are you feeding your rabbit? Diet is another factor linked to aggression, and is something which must be changed if necessary. Rabbits that are fed a high protein pellet food can often have aggressive tendencies due to the rocket-fuel like food they are consuming. Remember, rabbits were designed to eat grass, grass and more grass and must be fed a primarily hay based diet (see feeding section for more details) Providing a diet based on hay certainly helps with the final factor that influences aggression.

Could your rabbit be bored? Rabbits in the wild are highly active, sociable creatures that will spend at least eight hours a day eating. In captivity, many rabbits are kept in barren, unfurnished hutches and fed a commercial diet that is consumed in a matter of minutes; this is a very boring existence. Few people would be surprised at a cat becoming stir-crazy if kept in a rabbit hutch yet **are** surprised when their rabbit starts to show signs of boredom related stress and aggression. By providing a hay based diet, your rabbit will spend longer eating and have less time to become bored. It is important that toys such as natural branches from safe fruit tress are provided to amuse your pet when you are not around. Known as environmental enrichment, providing an ever changing selection of things to do is a system used by zoos across the world to keep their animals as mentally engaged as possible and is easily replicated with your pets. You must also be committed to ensuring you spend time with you rabbit, allowing it the freedom of the house or garden as often as possible.

TTouch is very useful when combating aggression but you must always ensure that any other factors are taken into consideration. A rabbit that is given TTouch but still kept on a poor diet in a barren cage is unlikely to change its behaviour for too long. In order for TTouch to be truly effective with these rabbits it is important to start in a confined neutral area such as a clean carrier.

Start by using paint brushes or feathers to initiate interaction with your rabbit by gently stroking its head through the bars of the carrier, and watch your rabbit's reaction. If your rabbit lunges at the tools then it is showing a fear of contact with people, yet if your pet seems unfazed by this contact then it would suggest your pet has more of a fear of being picked up. Rabbits that accept the use of tools will often learn to accept being touched with the hands in a very short space of time.

This rabbit is showing genuine curiosity towards the TTouch wands. This would indicate that he has a fear of being picked up rather than a fear of people.

Use a paintbrush to make small one and a quarter circles on the forehead, base of the ears and on the cheeks. Stroking the whiskers against the face is very reassuring and helps to stimulate the rabbit to breathe deeply, which is calming in itself. It is important to start on the head area as this is usually the least threatening area for a rabbit to be touched. The sides and back end are used in ritualised aggression between rabbits and therefore this area is not a good starting point for touching an aggressive rabbit. After each circle, ensure you slide to a new area to make the next TTouch. After making a few circles, move away and give your rabbit a few minutes to process the information it has received. It can be handy to have some tasty vegetables in the carrier for the rabbit to eat. Repeat this circling and moving away until you feel your rabbit is ready to be touched with your hand. It may be that it takes several sessions on several days before you feel your rabbit is feeling happy for you to touch it and this is perfectly fine. It is far better to take the process slowly than to try to rush things. When it is ready, start to make gentle Llama TTouches (with the back of your hand) and watch your rabbit's reaction. If it reacts badly, don't worry, simply take a step back and use the tool once more. If it seems unfazed, begin to make small Chimp TTouches on the forehead and shoulders. In time, move on to using the front of your hand to make Clouded Leopard TTouches on the shoulder and Ear TTouches on the ears. End with Noah's

March but only stroke the areas you have previously been TTouching as to stroke your rabbit's hind end at this point could undo the trust you have built so far.

This process can then be repeated in the rabbit's home territory, start with the tools and take it slowly. The initial work outside of the rabbit's home territory is often enough to make this second phase far easier.

Rabbits that will not accept the use of tools or those that will but get stressed when touched with a hand may benefit from experiencing hands on TTouches through a towel or fleece. With your rabbit safely in a top opening carrier or box, slide a towel over the opened top so that it drapes over the sides effectively creating a false lid to the carrier.

Next, gently slide the towel down and over your rabbit, ensuring its head remains covered. The darkness that this affords your pet is comforting and allows you to safely start to give a variety of TTouches through the towel. By working through the towel, the contact is far less threatening than without, it also keeps the rabbit calm and you safe. Start with some gentle Clouded Leopard TTouches around the head and shoulders, move away and give your rabbit a few minutes to process the information. Return and give a few more Clouded Leopard TTouches and add in a few Abalone TTouches and Python Lifts on the shoulders. End with Noah's March but only stroke the areas you have previously been TTouching. As a rule, touching a rabbit's hind end can be seen as a sign of aggression and can cause a rabbit to act defensively. Aggressive rabbits tend to have large areas of tension, especially in the hindquarters that can be soothed with various TTouches but always take things nice and slowly. Keep a positive image in mind and gently talk to your rabbit throughout.

TRAINING TIP

Is it really necessary to reach into your pet's enclosure and pick it up? Many rabbits, even well socialised ones, have a fear of being picked up when in an enclosed space; it is perfectly understandable. It is far kinder to teach your pet to hop into a carrier so it can be transported, to its outside run for example. You can train your pet to hop into a carrier by placing tasty treats inside and NEVER forcing your pet to enter. In this way, your pet soon learns that the carrier is a safe place to be. It also means that your rabbit is far more likely to initiate contact, looking for affection. They soon learn that any close contact with you is a good thing as it is never forced on them.

Chewing household objects and/or tearing wallpaper.

Why does it occur?

Rabbits love to chew, it's in their nature. In the wild, rabbits would eat a wide range of tough objects such a tree bark and roots, their teeth are open rooted, meaning they grow continually throughout the rabbit's life. These special teeth, which grow at the rate of around 3 millimetres a day, are specially designed for the wear and tear of a rabbit's fibrous diet. In a household environment, rabbits do not have the same access to roots and bark but are spoiled with a wide array of items to chew instead. Many rabbit owners find furniture; clothes, telephone wires and even walls and wallpaper all succumb to their rabbit's sharp teeth.

There are three major causes for excess or inappropriate chewing:

- Hormones, especially with un-speyed female rabbits, neutering helps to diminish the desire to chew

- Boredom. Rabbits that are not provided with sufficient stimulation, especially if kept singly, will do their utmost to make their own entertainment i.e. chewing!

- Lack of training. Unless your rabbit is taught which items are suitable for chewing and which are out of bounds, it will simply assume that your Prada shoes are no different from a specially provided chew toy!

What can I do to help?

Excessive chewing or chewing the incorrect objects must be tackled with a three pronged approach, however, you must understand that rabbits will be rabbits and a degree of chewing is always likely. If you have a house-rabbit or when bringing your rabbit indoors to play, you MUST ensure that the house/room is bunny-proof, i.e. all items that you do not wish to be chewed MUST be removed. Even more importantly, ANY electrical cables must be out of reach or encased in a hard plastic cable cover. Curiosity, when it comes to cables, really could kill the rabbit.

In order to minimise chewing, your pet must first be neutered. Neutering helps to reduce the hormones surging through your pet's body and in turn, helps to reduce the desire to chew. Female rabbits, if left un-speyed, have a strong burrow building instinct, which includes the chewing of objects she feels are in her way. This is similar to her job in the wild, as she would need to remove roots that cross her tunnels.

The second factor to consider is boredom. Rabbits need mental stimulation to prevent them from making their own fun by destroying your belongings. Known as environmental enrichment, creating a fun and stimulating environment is essential part of pet ownership. You must be sure to provide a variety of objects to ensure your rabbit's needs are met. Many people supply a variety of chew toys but find their rabbit pays them no attention; in human terms, this can be equated to having a whole library of books all on one subject. You may love reading, but the novelty will be sure to run out swiftly.

Rabbits show a range of different play behaviours and these should be taken in to account when providing toys. These include digging, chewing, shredding, rolling, throwing, climbing and nest building.

Now you do not need to spend a fortune on expensive toys for your pet as they can easily and cheaply be home made. Cardboard boxes with a hole cut in the side will provide an opportunity to climb and dig, an old yellow pages can be given to shred (remove if your rabbit is seen to ingest the paper, most however just scatter this on the floor!) untreated apple branches can be given to chew (make these as plentiful as you can) light-weight plastic flower pots can be rolled and thrown whilst toilet paper tubes have endless uses, especially when stuffed with hay. As long as the toy is safe, let your imagination run wild!

The third point to consider is training your pet to differentiate between *its* toys and *your* belongings. The success in training your pet will depend on its personality and you may have a few hurdles along the way. The biggest chewers tend to be very outgoing, hyperactive rabbits and these in turn tend to be very intelligent. However, with this intelligence comes the ability to challenge authority and you may find that these rabbits occasionally feel the need to push the boundaries. If you find your rabbit chewing something it shouldn't, make a distraction by clapping your hands. This is not designed to scare the rabbit but to momentarily distract it from chewing. As soon as the rabbit stops, offer it a more appropriate chew item and give plenty of praise when it does chew the correct object.

Once your rabbit gets the hang of this, you can add in a trigger word "LEAVE" at the same time as giving the clap signal. Over time, your pet will learn not to chew certain objects and you will also be able to remove the hand clapping and just use the word "LEAVE" instead. This is always a useful tool, especially if you have guests which leave tasty coats and handbags within easy reach!

<u>Rabbit leaves small piles of dry faecal droppings in certain locations, especially doorways. Some may have been bitten in half.</u>

Why does it occur?

Rabbits are territorial creatures and love the joys of home. Just like people, they can become concerned about strangers coming in uninvited and feel the need to take precautions to prevent this from happening. We are lucky enough to be able to lock our front doors and windows or set intruder alarms; our rabbits do not have this luxury and therefore use droppings instead. Rabbits have a very good sense of smell and use droppings to convey all sorts of information from sex to age and even stress levels. By placing these droppings in obvious locations your rabbit is simply saying "KEEP OUT!" to any passing rabbits. If you have more than one rabbit kept separately, especially if they are the same sex then this behaviour is likely to be even more prevalent. Some rabbits go as far as to bite the dropping in half to ensure it smells as pungent as possible to anyone who is passing. Luckily, they are generally odourless to our noses but they are a tad unsightly. Un-neutered rabbits are generally far more territorial and often back up their messages with urine, just to make sure they get their point across.

Which TTouches may help?

Abalone, Python Lift, Raccoon.

What can I do to help?

Cracking this territorial behaviour can be very tricky indeed as it is such a natural behaviour for rabbits to exhibit. It is likely that all rabbits show this behaviour to a degree. The first consideration is to be sure that the droppings are round, dry and generally odourless. If the droppings are squashy, sticky, and smelly or found flat and trodden into the carpet, then you are actually looking at cecotropes instead. These are the droppings that your rabbit should be eating as soon as they are produced. This is a behaviour that evolved from a need to eat poor quality food and is similar to the way cows chew the cud. If these droppings are the problem then your pet's diet must be reviewed as they may be consuming too much protein or they may in fact be only eating certain parts of their mixed food.

Provided the droppings are of the correct type and appear to deliberately being left in these incorrect areas, then you must ensure your pet is neutered. Hormones play a big factor in the placement of territorial droppings and neutering often results in a marked decrease in this behaviour. TTouch can help to build the rabbit's self-confidence which in turn can help to reduce this territorial behaviour. A little like aggression, it can stem from a form of insecurity as your rabbit feels the need to protect itself from all comers. For persistent offenders, it can be useful to provide a litter tray near to the area they are using. However, as a rule, it is unlikely that territorial marking will stop altogether so keeping a dustpan and brush handy will be a good bet!

Rabbit is either not getting on with its current cage mate or will not bond to a new partner that it is introduced to.

Why does it occur?

Contrary to the belief that all rabbits are advocates of free love, rabbits can be very tricky when it comes to social introductions. In the wild, many rabbits will in fact mate for life and only find a new partner if their original mate dies. Rabbit social structure is very complex and finding an appropriate partner can be a tricky prospect; that isn't to say you shouldn't try, far from it in fact. Rabbits NEED the company of their own kind and can have many behavioural problems if kept singly.

The key to helping two rabbits get along is a combination of finding a compatible partner, ensuring both partners are neutered and ensuring that they are introduced correctly. Generally speaking the best combination for a long-term partnership is a neutered male and female duo. Just like their wild counterparts, this combination works well; however many people have success with two males or two females provided they have grown up together.

It is feasibly possible to introduce two unrelated male or female rabbits but the success depends on the individual personality of those involved.

Some sociable rabbits will get on like a house on fire and do not mind the sex of their cage mate, whereas others will simply never tolerate another rabbit of the same sex. Neutering is essential for all parties as this removes the sexual urges that can cause conflict. Once both parties have been neutered for a couple of weeks and their hormones have subsided, introductions can take place.

Which TTouches may help?

Raccoon TTouch and Ear TTouch

What can I do to help?

Take both rabbits and place them in a pet carrier that is large enough that they are comfortable, but snug enough that both rabbits are in bodily contact. It is important that they are both facing the same way. The best carrier for this purpose is an all wire carrier with a hinged top. When both rabbits are in the carrier, start by using small Raccoon TTouches on the head and Ear TTouches on the ears of both rabbits at the same time (this can be a little tricky so you may wish to practise on a friend or family member beforehand)

Ideally both rabbits should remain in the carrier for about half an hour to allow enough time for them to become acquainted in a very controlled environment. Provided no fighting has taken place, after at least half an hour, allow both rabbits to hop out of the carrier together into a large open area that neither has been to before. This could be a spare room in the house, or even the bathroom. It is VERY important that both rabbits be encouraged to hop out of the carrier at the same time and that they are not lifted out. By hopping out together, an unwritten agreement is made that neither party owns this territory. It is vitally important that this area is large enough to give them enough space to avoid each other yet be in constant view of each other. A hutch is NOT suitable.

Next, distract them with some very tasty greens, this helps to calm and reduce tension further. The act of chewing releases calming hormones and grazing body posture discourages aggression. Provide plenty of hay and food and leave the rabbits together to get acquainted further but always keep an eye out for fighting. It is important to realise what equates to fighting in rabbit society and what is simply normal behaviour as you do not want to separate the new pair unnecessarily; if you do, you will need to start the process all over again. A true fight between rabbits is shocking to see; both animals lock together in a squirming ball of teeth and claws, each tearing at the other with their sharp hind claws. However, chasing and pulling of the fur around the hind end is normal behaviour and should not be stopped; in fact, rabbits have extra-thick fur on their bottoms for this very reason.

The bonding process is generally very swift. To begin with, both rabbits are likely to steer well clear of each other with the odd squabble. After 24 hours, much of the squabbling should start to subside and you should notice the rabbits starting to get a little closer to each other. It is important not to disturb the process or to separate them. After 48 hours, most rabbits, if introduced correctly, are likely to be found snuggled up together as if they had always known each other. Don't be alarmed to find hair that has been shed overnight, provided both of the rabbits are in one piece, then the bonding is going well. Major fighting is only likely to occur in the first few minutes, if initial introductions have taken place in the morning and all is ok come the evening, then they can safely be left together overnight without worry.

If you have a pair of rabbits that are not learning to accept one another, even though they are of the opposite sex, neutered and introduced as already mentioned, there is always hope. Once you have the pair in the carrier together, place them on the back seat of the car and take them for a ten minute drive around the block. As crazy as this sounds, the stress of the journey often acts to speed up the initial bonding process as they both seek comfort in each other's company. It is also a good idea, in these more challenging cases, to increase the length of time they are kept in the carrier together to at least one hour to help give enough time for the ice to be broken between them. You can then continue the process as described earlier. This may sound like a cruel thing to do but provided the rabbits are in a wire sided carrier they should not overheat whilst together and although they will find this a little stressful, the long term benefits of finding a rabbit partner far outweighs the initial discomfort of the bonding process.

Common guinea pig behaviour problems

Guinea pig is aggressive and bites when it is picked up or when a hand enters it cage.

Why does it occur?

It is very rare for guinea pigs to be aggressive but like all animals, if they feel threatened or have had a bad experience in the past, some individuals will become aggressive. The main reason this is unusual is that most fearful guinea pigs will choose to run away when they are scared. As prey animals, an element of fear and mistrust is hard wired into their makeup and it only takes one bad experience either with the breeder or with a previous owner to set up a deep-set fear or aggression problem.

Guinea pigs also have very poor eyesight and are easily startled, some breeds, especially albino guinea pigs, can be almost blind. This means that they can be easily startled and must be approached with care and respect. It can be a good idea to talk to these individuals as you approach their cage, so they are aware you are coming.

Boredom has shown to effect the mental state of guinea pigs, especially if kept outside and especially if kept singly. Ideally you should always try to keep two guinea pigs together and if possible, keep them indoors where they can feel part of the family. A lonely existence in a box at the end of the garden is enough to make anyone aggressive, yet is all the more sad when it happens to a guinea pig as they are usually such trusting, gentle creatures.

A lack of consistent, positive interaction with people can also cause aggression as can various medical problems such as dental issues and if female, ovarian cysts. Ovarian cysts are bags of fluid that develop on the ovaries of female guinea pigs. They can grow very large and can have the knock on effect of causing sexual aggression. Generally, sexual aggression will just be shown towards cage mates but it has been known that guinea pigs affected with these cysts can become grumpy with people. It is possible to treat these cysts in a number of ways, firstly by having the guinea pig neutered or if too frail for such an operation by treating with injections of a hormone called HCG (human chorionic gonadotropin). This may shrink ovarian cysts but this is a temporary measure as they will often need draining or repeat treatments. Always seek advice from your vet who will be able to perform an ultra-scan to check if these are causing the problem.

<u>What can I do to help?</u>

TTouch is extremely effective in helping guinea pigs to reduce their aggressive tendencies but a full veterinary check is essential to rule out any medical reason for your pet's bad temper. Once your pet has a clean bill of health, begin by initiating contact with a paintbrush or feather, if your pet spins or lunges at the tool then you may need to use two; one to stroke and one as a distraction. Using your chosen tool, make gentle one and a quarter circles around the base of the ears and long gentle strokes over the body. Guinea pigs must be given lots of breaks between strokes as they can be easily overwhelmed. On occasion, the most effective technique is to give a two or three circles and/or strokes and then retreat. After a minute or so return and make a few more strokes and again retreat. Don't be too worried if your guinea pig continues to lunge when you start again, the key thing to notice is the length of time it takes him or her to settle. You are sure to notice your guinea pig becomes calm and settled far more quickly with each TTouch session until eventually it no longer feels the need to lunge.

During the sessions, remember to breathe by 'toning' to your guinea pig in a soothing voice. Once your guinea pig is happy with the use of the tools, you can then begin to introduce your hand in to the equation. Start by moving your hand down the paintbrush until you are almost touching them. Start to make slow and gentle Llama TTouches with the back of your hand, making slow and calm one and a quarter circles, by using the back of your hand; your guinea pig appears to recognise the fact that it is not going to be grabbed. Watch your guinea pig's reactions to see if it is content or stressed. You may need to have several sessions with tools before even thinking about the Llama TTouch but some guinea pigs overcome their fears very quickly. Once your guinea pig seems happy with this TTouch, move on to using the Chimp and Baby Chimp TTouches to make one and quarter circles around the head, shoulders and neck area, remembering not to make more than one TTouch on the same spot but sliding a centimetre or so away to make the next TTouch.

TRAINING TIP

Is it really necessary to reach into your pet's enclosure and pick it up? Many guinea pigs, even well socialised ones, have a fear of being picked up when in an enclosed space; it is perfectly understandable. It is far kinder to teach your pet to hop into a carrier so it can be transported, to its outside run for example. You can train your pet to hop into a carrier by placing tasty treats inside and NEVER forcing your pet to enter. In this way, your pet soon learns that the carrier is a safe place to be and will mean moving your pet from one place to another is far less stressful. . It also means that your guinea pig is far more likely to initiate contact, looking for affection. They soon learn that any close contact with you is a good thing as it is never forced on them.

Guinea pig panics and runs away at the very sound of you opening its cage door

Why does it occur?

Guinea pigs that have missed vital handling as babies will often be very skittish around people. The sight of an approaching hand can be very scary indeed to a nervous guinea pig. Instinct tells them that they should flee at the very sight or sound of the door opening; no conscious thought goes into this flight reaction. This flight reaction would have served them well in a wild environment as it would have helped them to avoid predators, in a captive situation however, it causes unnecessary stress and can result in injury.

Which TTouches may help?

Clouded Leopard, Ear and Raccoon TTouches plus the use of TTouch tools and Mouth work.

What can I do to help?

In order for a guinea pig to overcome its fear of people it is necessary to contain it in a soft towel or fleece. Guinea pigs that have had little contact with people are often so terrified that the use of TTouch tools can be a tricky affair, even if contained in a carrier, as you run the risk of the guinea pig panicking and dashing back and forth. This only serves to increase their stress levels and hinders any positive learning. In order to make this easier and more stress free for you and your guinea pig, it would be best to encourage them into a top opening carrier. Once in the carrier, slide a towel or fleece over the opened top and allow it to drape over the sides, creating a false lid. Gently and slowly drape this towel over the guinea pig and wrap it in a bundle. You must get the pressure just right. Too tight and you risk injuring the guinea pig, too loose and it might panic.

One of the wonders of the TTouch movements, is that they can still be effective when experience through a towel or fleece. Nervous pets may find direct hand contact or contact with a tool, too much to bear. However they often readily accept being TTouched through a towel or fleece without becoming concerned.

Once your guinea pig is bundled up, safely transfer it to your lap. It would be a nice idea to have a cushion on your lap to pop the guinea pig on to; this will help it feel more supported underfoot. Allow your guinea pig to remain covered but with all its feet on the cushion, begin to give calming Clouded Leopard and tiny Raccoon TTouches all over its body, talking calmly in a soothing voice. It is important to keep these sessions very short as guinea pigs cannot take too much at once.

Over time, you may feel comfortable enough to slide a paintbrush under the towel to make some small circles around the face and head and eventually may be able to introduce a tasty treat for them to nibble on. The act of eating helps to speed up the process of learning and engages the conscious brain. These scared guinea pigs can also benefit from having very tiny one and a quarter circles made on their mobile lips with a wet cotton bud (or Q-tip) or a finger as the lips are linked directly to the limbic area of the brain. This is a primitive part of the brain that is linked to the emotions. Use your finger to make tiny one and a quarter circles all over the ears too. Don't be disheartened if it takes some weeks to overcome this fear, some guinea pigs will never get over their phobias totally but through the use of TTouch, their fear can be managed and kept to a minimum.

TTouching the mouth of any pet can be dangerous. If you are afraid your pet may bite, please use caution and consider using a tool instead.

Common gerbil behaviour problems

Gerbil digs continually in the corner of the tank

Why does it occur?

The reasoning for this behaviour has been debated for many years but there are two main theories behind it. Firstly many people believe that this is a stereotypical behaviour. A stereotypical behaviour is a repetitive or ritualistic movement or posture thought to come about due to a lack of stimulation or opportunity to behave in a natural way. This behaviour is well documented and understood in animals that are kept in cramped and cruel conditions such as battery hens or lions kept in zoos, but can the same be said for captive gerbils?

It is true that some people keep their gerbils in totally unsuitable housing that is barren and un-stimulating and it would be understandable for their gerbils to show this form of behaviour. However many people keep their gerbils in wonderfully thought-out environments and still have the same issue. It is interesting to note that very young gerbils can often show this behaviour soon after leaving the nest which suggests that there may be differing factors involved.

The second school of thought is to do with the experiences or lack of them that baby gerbils encounter while still in the nest. A recent study found that gerbils that are raised in an enclosed nesting box with an entrance tunnel do not develop this stereotypical behaviour. Equally, even if the parents have not been raised this way and therefore do show this behaviour, the young do not learn the behaviour from the parents. It would seem that in the wild, the young would help to develop the burrow system if it were needed; when raised without an enclosed nest box or even with nest box without a tunnel entrance, the desire to build is overwhelming and becomes a stereotypical behaviour. This behaviour quickly affects the way in which the brain develops meaning that stereotypical digging is very hard to prevent in adulthood.

What can I do to help?

Although it can be hard to stop this behaviour, as they are such intelligent and hyperactive creatures, you must provide your gerbil with an enriching environment with plenty of toys, safe natural branches and cardboard boxes. These are often enough to keep your gerbils occupied and to take their minds off digging as much as possible.

Difficulty in introducing unrelated gerbils

Why does it occur?

Gerbils must always be kept with company of their own kind wherever possible and two same sex littermates make the perfect combination. However, whether through rescuing a lone gerbil or one of a pair passing away, occasionally you may find yourself with a single gerbil. It is certainly possible to introduce a new gerbil to an existing one but gerbils are very territorial so you must be prepared to work very hard to ensure they learn to love each other. Two unrelated male gerbils are usually easier to introduce than two females but care must always be taken.

Which TTouches may help?

TTouches with tools and Raccoon TTouch

What can I do to help?

The safest method of introducing two unrelated gerbils is to use the split tank method but there is one important fact to consider – it cannot be guaranteed that both gerbils will get along, some simply will not tolerate a new companion. You must make provisions to keep both gerbils separately if need be.

Using wire mesh attached to a wooden frame, split the gerbil tank into two. The wooden frame must be secure so neither gerbil can get into the other's side and the holes in the mesh must be small enough to prevent fighting through the wire; you may need to double up the mesh just in case. Keep each gerbil in a separate side of the mesh, remembering to provide each gerbil with its own food and water bottle. Keep toys to a minimum but remember to provide sufficient bedding.

TTouch can be used to help speed up the bonding process. Start by using two artists paintbrushes to TTouch both of the gerbils at the same time. This can be a little tricky to master especially as gerbils are such mobile little creatures but practice does make perfect. Make small Raccoon TTouches around the head and face and try to circle the base of the ears if you can. TTouching two animals at once may seem a strange concept but experience with many different species has shown that it is very effective at speeding the bonding process. It seems a connection is made between the two animals before they meet and hostility is reduced.

Every day, swap the gerbils into the other side, still keeping them separate. Watch their behaviour and keep a note of the way they are interacting with each other. Over time, the gerbils should get used to each other being around and grow to accept each other. When you notice the two making their nests next to the mesh and hopefully sleeping together, it is time to let them meet (be aware this can take weeks to get to this stage with some gerbils) Remove all tasty treats and toys from the cage so there is nothing to fall out over and then remove the partition. Ideally, introduce the pair in the same tank, as the newly formed clan smell can help with the bonding process, although do keep the tank pretty bare to avoid squabbles. If this fails, then an area of neutral territory can be tried.

Watch carefully for any signs of fighting over the next forty eight hours. If you notice them grooming each other or sleeping in the same nest, then you can safely say, mission accomplished!

Common hamster behaviour problems
Hamster runs away when you approach the cage or open the door

Why does it occur?

Hamsters that run away at the very sign of their human guardian are scared and reacting just like they would at the sign of a predator. Hopefully you have no desire to consume your hamster but sadly it doesn't know this and isn't willing to take the chance. Fear can come about for a number of reasons but there are two that stand out:
- Your hamster may have had a very bad experience with the breeder or pet shop and now believes all people are a threat
- Your hamster may have had very little handling or socialisation, and therefore has no idea if people are friend or foe. Understandably, assuming you are foe is definitely the safer option as far as your hamster is concerned.

If your hamster was purchased from a pet shop, there is a likelihood that they have been bred at a rodent farm. These farms breed hamsters on a huge scale and make no attempt to socialise their young, the only experience they have had of people is the journey from the breeder to the pet shop, this is enough to put any hamster off getting to know human kind.

Which TTouches may help?

Using TTouch tools

What can I do to help?

Teaching your hamster not to fear people is definitely possible but you must have patience and ensure you take the process slowly. Luckily, hamsters are greedy little things who love to eat; therefore tasty treats can be very useful in persuading your hamster to trust you, especially when combined with the TTouch tools. Start by using a soft paintbrush to gently stroke the bars of your hamster's cage for a few moments and then retreat. Repeat this stroking and retreating for five minutes. Stroking the bars of the cage may seem like a crazy thing to do, but it would seem that the hamster experiences a feeling of connection to you but at the same time feels safe in the knowledge that the door is still closed. Next, use the paintbrush to stroke the hamster through the bars of the cage for a few moments and retreat. Repeat this four times and then give the hamster a break, maybe until the following evening. Even if the hamster is seemingly responding very well to this, it is very important not to push things too far. The last thing you want to do is confirm your hamster's fear and cause it to become even more scared.

The following day, approach once more with the tool and note your hamster's reaction. Many will now show curiosity and seem far calmer than they were the previous day. The next step is to open the cage door and once again, stroke the cage bars, be sure to watch your pet's reaction. Does it show signs of fear and panic or seem calm? Provided it remains calm, approach slowly with the paintbrush and make small circles and strokes around the head, neck and shoulders for thirty seconds and then retreat. Give your hamster a two minute break and repeat. Should it appear scared, take a step back and return to stroking the cage bars and retreating, remember, there is no rush.

Repeat this process over the next few nights and your hamster will become calm in your presence. The temptation to pick up your hamster must be avoided as it is important for trust to develop before-hand. The next step is to offer your hamster a tasty treat on the floor of the cage with your hand inside the cage at the same time. If your hamster is happy to take the treat, move on to laying your hand on the floor of the cage, next to the treat.

Again, once your hamster is happy to take the treat, move to having the treat on the flat of your hand, resting on the cage floor. Remain still and the hamster will soon climb onto your hand to collect it. Repeat this last stage until you are able to gently lift your hand without worrying the hamster. Eventually, you will be able to lift your hand, complete with hamster, out of the cage, however, always ensure that you have the cage on the floor to do this, just in case it jumps off. A fall can easily injure your pet.

Another, kinder option is to teach your hamster to crawl into a tube whilst in the cage. The tube (with hamster inside) can then be lifted out of the cage and onto a soft surface. When it is time for your hamster to go back into its cage, the process can be repeated. It is a good idea to have some tasty food in the cage for your hamster, that way they do not resent being put away. Hamsters are clever little creatures and they soon learn that a tube represents travelling somewhere and that the destination offers a reward; the reward being freedom and fun when coming out of the cage and tasty food when going back in.

Hamster bites and is aggressive during the day but fine in the evening

Why does it occur?

Hamsters are naturally nocturnal and LOVE to sleep; if you wake your hamster whilst it is sleeping it is likely to be just a little peeved at the disturbance.

What can I do to help?

It is important to avoid waking your hamster unnecessarily but there are times when you will need to (I'm sure if you were to take your hamster to the veterinarian at three in the morning the bill would be shocking!) Calmly wake your hamster from its slumber, talking in a quiet and soothing voice. As your hamster wakes, take some very tasty food and leave it away from the bed so your hamster must get up to get it. Once it seems fully awake, you can now safely retrieve your pet.

Hamster chews the cage bars continually

Why does it occur?

If your hamster chews the cage bars, it is likely that it is simply bored and under stimulated. Hamsters in the wild would spend all night foraging, potentially walking up to three miles in search of food. In the confines of a cage, this simply isn't possible and many will show these signs of stress. The minimum cage size for a Syrian hamster is at least three foot long; many pet shop cages are simply far, far too small. Bar chewing can become a learned behaviour and therefore, once it starts, there is a fair chance the behaviour will continue to some degree even when the hamster is moved to larger and more stimulating surroundings.

What can I do to help?

Prevention is far better than cure, but the idea is the same. You must provide your pet with as much enrichment as possible. Provide toys and natural fruit branches, safe meadow hay and even a sand bath with chinchilla sand for digging in. The more toys you can provide along with a large enough cage, the better. Look to enrich your hamster's cage in as many new and innovative ways as you can. Scatter feeding your pet (sprinkling food into the bedding and onto its toys) especially with millet seed as a treat, is a great way of making your pet work for its meal and hanging pieces of apple from the bars will provide much needed stimulation.

Common mouse behaviour problems

Mice are generally very problem free creatures provided they are handled gently and calmly, however, male mice can have behavioural troubles due to elevated hormone levels. This can show itself as aggression to people and other male mice.

What can I do to help?

The best way to help an aggressive, hormonal male mouse is castration. With the increased safety of anesthetics, the process of castration for male mice is far easier than ever before, provided you find an experienced veterinarian. Once castrated, hormone levels subside, along with the territorial aggression so common in these individuals. Equally, mice love company but often fall out with their male counterparts. Castration creates calmer individuals that can be introduced to a group of female mice with little problem. In fact, male mice can help to stabilize a group of female mice and help to bring about balance. A word of warning though, do make sure you wait at least 8 weeks after castration to be sure that the male is unable to father any offspring.

Common rat behaviour problems

Rat is aggressive

Why does it occur?

Aggression in rats is a complicated subject and has many different possible causes. In order to find out what is causing your rat to become aggressive you must look at every aspect of its environment and the circumstances surrounding the aggression. Fear, poor eyesight, hormonal or territorial issues, pain and boredom can all cause rats to show aggression

Firstly, can your pet see? This may sound like a crazy question but many rats with pink or ruby eyes (not just albino) have very poor eyesight. If this is the case, be sure to speak to your pet calmly as you approach in order to give it some warning that you are around. Do not grab these rats or touch them when they are unaware.

If they are healthy, then the biting is likely to be fear related due to experiences in early life (if young), through bad handling or through a lack of socialisation. Socialisation is the period in which an animal learns to accept people being part of day to day life. This allows them to trust in people and not be afraid. If rats are left to their own devices without any human contact, they can become terrified of anything other than other rats. In a confined environment, this fear often manifests itself as aggression. Similarly, rats which have been subject to abuse or bad handling can soon learn that people are not quite as nice as they once thought.

Many rats will suffer from territorial biting; meaning they are lovely outside of their cage but will attack whilst confined in their cage. This behaviour is usually seen in entire males but only occasionally in females. Castration can certainly help in reducing the behaviour if the rat is male but the cage size and enrichment must always be considered.

Boredom is very stressful and rats that are kept in cramped, barren conditions can become very territorial, simply because they have nothing better to do and are somewhat institutionalized.

Which TTouches may help?

Using TTouch tools

What can I do to help?

Obtaining a much larger cage and providing an array of fun toys will certainly be of benefit. Make sure to get a cage with large enough doors to allow you to spot clean the cage whilst respecting your rat's privacy.

Territorial rats should be managed differently from other rats and must be allowed to come out of their cages of their own accord. If we forcibly take them out of their cages then you risk reinforcing their territorial behaviour. Paintbrushes can be used to stroke and make circular TTouches through the bars and opened door. In doing so, the rat learns to remain calm when the door opens and that attacking will not cause the 'intruder' to leave. Often this territorial behaviour is instinctive and by introducing the TTouch circular movements, you can help your rat to act rather than react, in other words, to think about the situation and realise that there is no need to be aggressive.

If your pet bites in all circumstances then a full veterinary check up is essential as, like all pets, rats will bite when in pain. Providing all is well, begin working with TTouch tools such as paintbrushes and feathers, stroking around the head and face; this is very effective in developing trust. Make tiny circular Ear TTouches around the base of the ears and stroke right from the base to the tip. If you are able to hold your pet, gently use the Tail TTouch by undulating the tail very gently and slowly circling the tail at the base. Many older male rats can become very stiff through the pelvis which can make them a little grumpy.

It may be worth considering removing any enclosed areas of the cage, for example a covered bed, to allow easier access to your rat. This may seem a little mean, but experience shows that progression is slower when they are continually cowering inside an igloo.

Chapter 10 – When the end comes

<u>Every life that ever forms, or ever comes to be,
touches the world in some small way for all eternity.</u>

Making the decision to put your beloved small pet to sleep is never an easy one. Just because they are small in stature does not mean the impression they leave on their human guardian is by any means small. In fact, for many children, the death of the family hamster may be their first experience of this sad fact of life.

The decision is not one to take lightly and it is important that your veterinarian agrees. However, be sure that they are not persuading you to put your animal to sleep for financial reasons. Some vets see small animals as disposable pets and will often suggest euthanasia as the first option over treatment. In this day an age this is quite frankly a shocking attitude to life, as I believe the life of the pet should be put first at all times. If an operation is unlikely to succeed and the animal will endure undue suffering then, euthanasia is best. However, if the operation is feasible and the animal is fit enough to recover well, then euthanasia is not the best option.

If euthanasia has been decided upon, all things considered, then you will want the end to be as pain free and kind as possible. Euthanasia for small pets is tricky and is approached in a different way to cats and dogs. Dogs and cats are put to sleep with an injection administered into a vein, this is generally pain free and the animal slips quietly away. Rabbits are fortunate enough to have a large vein running through their ears and will be able to be put to sleep in this manner also. With our smaller pets, this is not the case as their veins are too small for an injection to be given this way; instead, an injection is often made directly into the heart. This is usually a quick ending; however, if the injection is given in this way, the pain and distress the animal has to endure is, in my view unacceptable. Many pets, especially rats and guinea pigs, are known to squeal loudly, which any pet owner is sure to see as a sign of distress. Although the ending is a quick one, I personally would not want my small pet's last moments to be painful and full of distress.

As an alternative, many vets choose to inject the animal into the abdomen; this can be a humane and pain free method if given by an experienced and confident vet. Unfortunately many vets choose to use needles which are of too large a gauge and therefore cause unnecessary discomfort when injected. Ideally a very fine insulin syringe should be used. Equally, the injection must be given correctly; ideally the injection is given on the lower right side of the abdomen to avoid the major organs.

Even with the most confident and experienced vet, having an injection of any sort can be painful and is equally distressing for the owner of the pet as well. With this in mind, many pet owners insist on having their small friend sedated prior to the injection being made. I personally agree this is a kind thing to do, but once again there are different ways of doing so:
- Gaseous sedation
- Injectable sedation

If sedation is given in the form of gas, your pet may either be placed in a sealed box with a flow of anesthetic gas being pumped in or with a face mask. You must check with your Veterinarian to ensure they are using an anesthetic gas and oxygen mix, not just anesthetic. Even though these are the final moments of your pet's life, if placed in a box without oxygen, this can be very distressing for your pet. On the flip side, some pets can jump around wildly if the oxygen content is too high so the balance must be correct.

If an injectable sedative is used, this is generally given in the scruff of the neck with a fine syringe. Many pets hardly notice this injection and although it can take a few minutes to take effect, most small animals are sound asleep within five to ten minutes. During this time, your vet will allow you to cuddle and sooth your pet.

Once your pet is sedated, most will need a final injection, preferably in the abdomen, to put them to sleep. As they are sedated, they will not feel the injection and most slip peacefully away.

During the whole process, it can be lovely to give your pet its favourite TTouches. In this way, you help to calm and soothe both your pet and yourself.

It can be hard to think about ending your small pet's life but it is something that every small pet owner is likely to face at some point. Our small pets are simply not designed to get old as in the wild they would usually become prey for another animal as they start to slow down. However, in captivity the level of care and availability of food results in our small pets living far longer than their wild cousins. Having an animal put to sleep is one of the hardest decisions to make however, in many ways it is also the bravest and kindest thing you can do for your pet if they are suffering.

Don't be afraid to cry, losing any animal is a heartbreaking moment, and just because they are smaller doesn't mean the impact of their death is any less distressing. Many people find it hard to contemplate how losing a small pet feels. With this in mind there are many pet bereavement organizations available and many are completely free of charge.

Adam is a qualified Tellington TTouch Companion Animal practitioner, working on a one to one basis with private clients and teaching one day workshops. He has written for many national and international magazines on many animal behaviour and welfare issues. He is a stoic campaigner for improvements in animal welfare and believes the lives are our smaller pets can be improved through greater knowledge and understanding.

Adam can be contacted by visiting his website:
www.animals-at-ease.co.uk
Or by email:
thebigguidetosmallpets@animals-at-ease.co.uk

Contact list and useful sources of information

Animals at Ease – The website for the author, Adam Rogers
www.animals-at-ease.co.uk
The official Tellington TTouch website.
www.TTouch.com
The UK TTouch and TTeam Centre.
www.TTouchTTeam.co.uk
Rescue Helpers Unite – A fantastic website bringing rescued animals and potential new owners together.
www.rescuehelpersunite.co.uk
Fancy Rats – A website full of information and a thriving forum for all things rat related.
www.fancy-rats.co.uk
E-Gerbil – A great source of gerbil related information.
www.egerbil.com
All about mice – As the name suggests, this website is dedicated to the care of mice.
www.allaboutmice.co.uk
The House Rabbit Association - This fantastic website is a must for rabbit owners.
www.rabbit.org
The Southern Hamster Club – A fantastic website with great information and contacts for all things hamster related.
www.southernhamsterclub.co.uk

Acknowledgments and thanks

Before I go any further I'd like to say a HUGE thank you to everyone who I have forgotten to mention. Those that know me will say what a terrible memory I have and with this in mind there are bound to people I have forgotten. To those unfortunate few, thank you, thank you, thank you for all your help and support and please don't take it personally!

My most important thank you has to go to all the animals that have come into my life over the years. To Squidgy my now departed canine companion, soul mate and best friend, you may be gone but will never be forgotten. Thank you for teaching me just what true love and devotion truly looks like. We'll meet again one day old friend.

Animals, even so called 'problem animals' all have something to teach us and each and every one leaves a lasting imprint on the soul. The list of animals I would like to thank would take a whole other book to mention but rest assured they have all inspired me to dedicate my life to improving the lives of these often neglected creatures.

To my ever-patient Mother, Pat. Thank you for devoting so much time to endlessly proof read time and time again after every mind change and amendment, your spot on grammatical suggestions and for your wonderful head teacher wisdom. I couldn't have done it without you. Thank you also for putting up with the endless stream of small furries that have graced our doors over the years and for supporting my eccentric animal obsessions. My gratitude to you is beyond words.

Thank you to Robyn, Sarah, Lynda, Tina and all of the TTouch family for their magical inspiration and support and for helping me to realise I'm not such a loon for writing a book on this subject. TTouch has given me such a wonderful outlook on our relationship with the natural world and the creatures whose lives we share. If just one person gains half of the joy and wonder TTouch has brought me, then writing this book has been worthwhile.

Thank you to Dorothy for so many of your wonderful hints and tips and for all the animal fun we have had over the years. Even driving up the M4 with a carload of rescued chickens was a pleasure with you for company! Thank you for confirming that each and every animal from the smallest mouse to the largest dog should be treated like the amazing, individual little beings they are.

Thanks must go to Shirley for allowing her menagerie to be the subjects of many of the photos in this book. I must have driven you crazy with endless hours of paparazzi style snapping!

Thanks also to Claire Marr for her level headed (at times!) outlook on life and for helping to guide me in the right direction.

Thank you to Edd Payton for your wonderful illustrations and for allowing the wonderful Pandora and Geronimo to be badgered for photos.

Thank you to Wendy Barry (aka the font of all hamster know how) for your advice, time and dedication to hamster welfare.

And lastly, a huge thank you to all the wonderful people who dedicate their lives to rescuing the millions of small animals that find themselves neglected at the hands of man. Without you, so many little lives would either be cut short or be so very neglected.